THE APPRENTICE

How to get hired not fired

Sir Alan Sugar

**LEARNING
RESOURCES
CENTRE**

HAVERING
COLLEGE

BBC
BOOKS

To accompany the Talkback Thames series produced for BBC TV

**Sir Alan Sugar is donating all his earnings
from sales of *The Apprentice* to charity.**

Published to accompany the Talkback Thames series produced for BBC TV.

First published in 2005 by BBC Worldwide Limited
Reprinted 2005
This revised and updated edition published in 2006

ISBN 0 563 49337 2

Published by BBC Books, BBC Worldwide Limited,
Woodlands, 80 Wood Lane, London W12 0TT

Commissioning editor: Nicky Ross
Editor and researcher: Sarah Sutton
Project editor: Eleanor Maxfield
Copy-editor: Patricia Burgess
Designer: Jo Ridgeway
Production controller: Peter Hunt

Photographs © Adam Lawrence
James Bainbridge (20–1), David Fraser/Frank PR (40)
© BBC/Talkback Thames

Set in Scala Sans
Printed and bound in Great Britain by Clays Ltd, St Ives plc

For more information about this and other BBC books,
please call 08700 777 001 or visit our website on www.bbcshop.co.uk

THE APPRENTICE

Sir Alan Sugar

ACKNOWLEDGEMENTS

This book could not have been written without the enthusiasm and assistance of the team at Talkback Thames. Particular thanks go to Cat Ledger for making it all possible, and to Alan Brown, Dan Adamson, Peter Moore, Tanya Shaw, Charlotte Wasserman, Alf Lawrie, James Bainbridge, Sophie Leonard, Emma Riley, Beth Dicks, Sharon Fuller and Sarah Holt. In addition, I would like to thank all the candidates in *The Apprentice* for their enthusiasm, dedication and willingness to undertake all the tasks.

The team at BBC Worldwide have done a highly professional job under the creative and focused leadership of Nicky Ross. Particular thanks go to Charlotte Lochhead, Trish Burgess, Ann Burnham, Ken McKay, Stuart Cooper and Eleanor Maxfield. Thanks also to Sarah Sutton.

Amongst my own highly respected team of colleagues and advisers I would like to acknowledge the professional help and involvement of my eyes and ears: Margaret Mountford and Nick Hewer; as well as my expert advisers: Bordan Tkachuk, CEO of Viglen, Claude Littner, Amstrad group adviser, and Paul Kemsley, founding director of Rock Investments. I'd also like to acknowledge the support and enthusiasm of my wife, Ann, who tolerated my absence over an extended period of time during the filming.

I'm glad to say no one was fired!

CONTENTS

WANTED

for *THE APPRENTICE*

Ambitious and hungry individuals:
Britain s brightest young business minds

Seven men — Seven women — One prize

All the winner has to do is survive
12 business tasks in the longest and
most exhilarating job interview ever.

REWARD

In exchange for demonstrating skill, talent,
motivation and business acumen, the winner
will get the chance to work for one year as
the Apprentice to Sir Alan Sugar and to earn
a six-figure salary working at the helm of
one of his companies.

PREFACE TO NEW EDITION

Filming the new series of *The Apprentice* has enabled me to revisit the first edition of the book of the series and flesh out the business bones of the core tasks. The challenge with a book based on a reality TV show is that it needs to be informative without giving away the result of the show. This new edition gives a fuller account of different team leaders' management styles, the challenges the teams face and the business-based reasons behind my firing decisions. The business tasks in this book are highly relevant to budding entrepreneurs and business people because they demonstrate core skills required in every company. The new edition is intended to add more meat to your armoury of skills.

The format of the programme is unchanged in the new series, but the candidates taking part, of course, are completely different. The themes of the tasks are also different. The mixture of personalities combined with the changed tasks will bring a new perspective to the show – and it's going to be an exciting and interesting series. I'll be focusing more on planning, organizing and leadership. Continued monitoring is what we're looking for: making sure that the project is staying on track.

In the world of business, as in life, everybody's different. Different people have different ways of going about things, but can end up reaching the same conclusion. That summarises business in a nutshell, and accounts for the success of *The Apprentice* as a television series too.

I'm often asked whether I will be looking for the same characteristics in this year's winner as I found in Tim Campbell – the Series 1 winner. Well, there's no guarantee of that. All I can say is may the best candidate win ... and I hope you enjoy following their path to success.

INTRODUCTION

Have you got what it takes?

The Apprentice began as a groundbreaking television programme, but I want it to bring out the entrepreneurial skills in every aspiring business pioneer. *The Apprentice* offers a virtual apprenticeship to business professionals and entrepreneurs alike.

I've been in business since I was a 12-year-old schoolkid really. If there was an opportunity and a demand I'd be there. It was an instinct, and gave me a buzz that has never left me. There are plenty of other young Sugars out there, and I want to help them to succeed.

The UK television series of *The Apprentice* has its roots in a highly successful American show of the same name, hosted by Donald Trump. The programme broke the mould of so-called 'reality' TV shows because it focuses on the world of business. We begin with a team of 14 candidates who are

Anyone who thinks that they can learn how to be an entrepreneur from a book will never be an entrepreneur.
SIR ALAN SUGAR

whittled down to a single finalist over a 12-week period. I am looking for someone with an eye for profit, a mind for new ideas, a flexibility of approach and a buzz of energy that means they are hungry and will have the determination to help me build a successful business. The interview process is created around tasks that focus on business: business decisions, commercial processes and the factors that lead to personal success or failure.

The Apprentice is a 12-week crash course in business survival techniques. Grounded in commercial reality, it is not for the faint-hearted. It doesn't claim to turn everyone into an entrepreneur, but if you've got what it takes, you'll recognize yourself and make the best of your natural ability as you read on.

What makes a good apprentice?

The skills of a good apprentice are epitomized by Tim Campbell, the first series' winner, and will no doubt be reflected in certain characteristics of future series' winners as well.

Tim was 27 when he became the preferred candidate for *The Apprentice*. With a BSc in Psychology and a Diploma from the Chartered Institute of Personnel and Development, on paper he did not stand out as a natural entrepreneur. After graduating from Middlesex University, Tim joined the graduate trainee programme at London Underground, became a specialist in management information and was responsible for delivering £5 million projects.

The true key to Tim's success probably lies more in his upbringing than his work experience. His background echoes my own in some respects, as he grew up in the East End of London. Brought up in a single-parent family and watching his mother work hard for her children's benefit, strengthened Tim's will to succeed. His self-confidence belies his youth. He's walked the rocky road from the streets of East Ham to the boardroom, and proved to his team-mates that he had the energy, self-belief and discipline to succeed.

Since becoming my apprentice, Tim has had an excellent first year and is getting on very well. He has worked very, very hard and he is a very good learner. The quality that has made him an ideal apprentice is his very quick, fast, absorbent brain. He only has to be told something once, he usually understands and remembers it, and he gets on with the task in hand. He is also eager to learn – which is a valuable and essential trait in an entrepreneur – and is quick to ask if he doesn't understand something, which I think is also very important. It means I can trust him not to make any maverick-style decisions that might jeopardize a project, and he will keep me informed of progress and other important matters.

With that kind of attitude and all those skills, he has turned out to be an excellent choice and a good fellow. But time will tell... He's a

very nice chap – and nice people don't always make successful busi-
nessmen.

Since he joined the company, Tim has been a project manager
with responsibility for managing the development and the launch of a
new face-care system. The way we operate is that every division has
access to a shared team of resources, particularly engineering, marketing and advertising. You can draw on the resources of the people
in these areas and use them for the amount of time that you want,
paying an internal fee for them or costing from your P&L (profit and
loss allocation). Tim has had access to those resources and has been
putting his project management skills to the test. The new product is
now being marketed exclusively on the Internet and combines online
marketing via Amstrad with franchise-style selling from home. I have
great confidence in the future of such marketing – and Tim's in
charge of that.

There is every chance that Tim will be with the company long
term. Like anybody else in my companies, he has a job for life if he
wants it. But he's not just there for the sake of *The Apprentice*; his division will need to continue to bring in money, and – like every other
employee – he'll have to continue to perform and deliver.

What s in it for you?

At heart I am a salesman – a salesman with a creative instinct and a nose for the marketplace. I never put a product into production without knowing what the marketplace wants, what features will make the product attractive to buyers, and what benefits there are to you, the customer, in parting with your hard-earned cash.

I've never been a great believer in business books or self-help books. I am a firm believer that if you've got what it takes, you'll have a feeling in your gut, a hunger in your belly – and you'll know you want to be your own boss.

But today's business world is full of challenges, and perhaps it's tougher to make a mark in a world full of high-street brands and big business deals than it was when I was starting out and doing deals along the Tottenham Court Road in London in the early 1970s.

So what's in it for you is the inside track. These pages will give you my thoughts on selling, marketing, self-management, team motivation and how to keep your eye focused on the bottom line.

It has taken me over 30 years to accumulate my knowledge and experience. I can offer you my own brand of business expertise. It will be short, sharp and from the hip. If it makes sense to you, then use it. If it doesn't, then don't try and do things my way. Whatever you do, be true to yourself and find your own style.

I'm not claiming to know it all, and don't ever call me a business guru because I'm still learning. It may sound like a cliché, but I learn something new every day.

The knowledge I have comes from the world of selling and manufacturing in electronics. In my field I am a successful businessman, and if my experience can help put an older head on young shoulders, then I am pleased to pass on what I know.

Born to lead or destined to follow?

Why is it that some employees remain technicians or project managers forever while others become innovative leaders, business creators and risk-takers who break the mould, reinvent the marketplace and create their own rules? The truth is, I don't know, but the 12 tasks in *The Apprentice* have been designed to reveal leadership qualities, sales skills, negotiation techniques and team-building ability. This means that these tasks will quickly show up those who haven't got what it takes to succeed in my business environment.

Why it is that some people are born to lead and others are better suited to supporting and project-delivery roles is a mystery. There's a need for all sorts in every business – but not in *The Apprentice*.

If you can't stand the heat in this business kitchen, there's only one thing to say...

You re fired!

chapter one

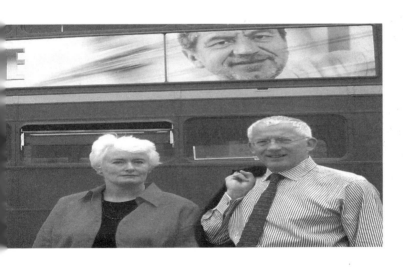

INTRODUCING THE BOARD

Sir Alan Sugar...

'Probably Britain's greatest entrepreneur.'

RUPERT MURDOCH
OWNER OF NEWS CORPORATION LTD

*'He's one of a new breed of British entrepreneurs.
I would like to see people like that as role models
for young people coming into business. I want
people to say, "Damn it, if he can do it, I can!"'*

LORD YOUNG
FORMER SECRETARY OF STATE FOR TRADE AND INDUSTRY
TALKING IN THE MID 1980S

I was very pleased to receive the recognition, quoted above, from Rupert Murdoch and Lord Young. I had worked hard to build my business, which by the mid 1980s had grown into a multi-million-pound corporation. What I want now is to inspire others – young and not so young – to do the same. I want people to follow their entrepreneurial instincts and become winners in business in their own right. I have been involved in the work of the Prince's Trust and other organizations focused on encouraging the development of personal business skills, especially among young people. I am at a stage in my business and in my life where 'putting something back' is important. *The Apprentice* offers the ideal opportunity to build on this aim, and I hope you enjoy and learn from the result.

I have a reputation for being blunt – a straight talker – and I'm not ashamed of that. Straight talking is honest. It gets to the point. Everyone is clear about what to expect. I don't mean to cause offence, but I won't suffer fools, especially if I have set my sights on a business goal. But I try to combine straight talking with integrity and straight dealing. It's important. Clients, staff and friends know they can trust me, and know that I have the courage of my convictions. I was looking for similar traits in our aspiring Apprentices.

So, is there a secret to being successful? If there were, you can be sure that the company I founded, Amstrad, would have found a way to sell it to the majority of the public by now at a price everyone could afford! However, after 30-odd years in the business I have learnt a thing or two, and it's time to pass that experience on.

Most job applications need a CV – even if you're headhunted, and even if you are the chairman of a company. There is always someone out there who wants to know who you are, what you're made of and what you're worth before they will consider doing business with you. I haven't applied for a job since I was a teenager, but my CV still opens doors and attracts business. Good CVs attract investors, help to build partnerships and tell people, loud and clear, who you are.

For the aspiring business person at a personal crossroads, a CV is also a way of taking stock and refocusing on who you are and where you're at. It's an audit of your achievements, skills and abilities.

I'm including some details from my own CV here so that you can understand my business path and have a context for what you'll be reading later in the book.

Sir Alan Michael Sugar

BORN: 24 March 1947

MARRIED: 1968 Ann Simons; two sons, one daughter, five grand-sons

ACHIEVEMENTS

- ☛ Main shareholder, chairman and chief executive of AMSTRAD
- ☛ Owner of Viglen
- ☛ 13 per cent shareholder of Tottenham Hotspur Football Club
- ☛ Owner of AMSHOLD (property and investment company)
- ☛ Owner of AMSAIR (executive jet aircraft for chartering)
- ☛ 55th on *The Times* Rich List (2005)

CHAIRMAN, AMSTRAD PLC SINCE FOUNDATION IN 1968

Amstrad plc will celebrate its fortieth anniversary in 2008. The company (Alan Michael Sugar TRADing) started as a small business enterprise and grew rapidly to become an international consumer electronics, telecoms and computer group with wholly owned subsidiaries in France, Germany, Benelux and Denmark, and a worldwide presence through a network of distributors. Stop anyone in the street and they will know the Amstrad name. This high level of brand awareness against giants such as Philips, Sony and IBM was achieved in a relatively short time. Amstrad was responsible for the phenomenal growth in the European personal computer market in the latter half of the 1980s, and was more recently the pioneer of the Europe-wide satellite receiving market.

A mobile telephone company, Dancall Telecom, purchased by Amstrad in 1994 for £6.4 million, was sold to Robert Bosch for £95 million in 1997.

Viglen Technology, a computer manufacturing company now known as Learning Technology, was floated separately on the London Stock Market in 1997, returning some £200 million to Amstrad shareholders. In 2003 that company was, effectively, purchased by my holding company and now operates as a private company based in the UK, and overseas through a subsidiary based in Hong Kong.

Amstrad, of which I hold nearly 30 per cent, is currently launching a series of high-technology, mass-market products on to the UK market.

CHAIRMAN, VIGLEN

I am chairman and majority shareholder in Viglen, one of Britain's largest manufacturers of personal computers. Established over 30 years ago, this company now focuses on the primary and secondary educational markets; it already supplies two-thirds of British universities.

With sales of around £100 million a year, the Viglen brand is now a supplier of choice to the broad educational sector.

CHAIRMAN, TOTTENHAM HOTSPUR PLC SINCE 1991

I became chairman of Premier League football club Tottenham Hotspur plc in June 1991, and retained that role until resigning in 2001. I remain the company's largest individual shareholder, with a 13 per cent stake. Since becoming involved in the national sport, I have made a significant impact as a commentator and, during my time as chairman, a Premier League motivator on the running and future direction of the game as far as broadcasting, youth policy, the Bosman ruling and financial disciplines are concerned.

AMSHOLD LTD

Amshold Ltd is my main holding company and is made up primarily of property companies that hold all my real estate interests.

COMMUNITY INTERESTS AND POSITIONS

- Honorary DSc, Brunel University
- Honorary DSc, City University Business School
- Appointed to Council of the Cranfield Institute
- Chairman of the governors, King Solomon High School, Redbridge
- Supporter of Business in the Community
- Founder and driving force behind the Excalibur Scholarship Scheme
- Honorary chairman, Bristol University Enterprise Centre

Responding to the call from Prime Minister John Major in 1993 to establish a new scheme for graduates from the old Eastern Bloc to study in Britain, I founded the Excalibur Scholarship Scheme. We recruited 21 other leading UK companies as sponsors, thus raising over £1 million. This has enabled more than 20 graduates from Central and Eastern Europe to enrol at British universities each year over the term of the scheme.

As an active supporter of many groups, I frequently address and advise young audiences on business subjects. In recent years I have visited over 20 cities, at the invitation of the chancellor of the exchequer, speaking to young people on the importance of business as a career.

CHARITABLE ACTIVITIES

The Alan Sugar Foundation, established in 1986, has donated millions of pounds to charity, including £1 million for the construction of an old people's home, £600,000 for the construction and upgrading of facilities at the Sinclair House day-centre for old and young in Redbridge, a contribution of £1.3 million to King Solomon High School in Redbridge, and nearly £1 million to the Great Ormond Street Hospital.

Most recently a donation of £1.3 million was made to rescue the Hackney Empire, which has now been restored. The foundation donates substantial amounts every year to an array of smaller, domestic charities orientated towards welfare. Additionally, I have raised £175,000 (through sponsorship) for the Muscular Dystrophy Group.

POLITICAL ACTIVITIES

- Supported and was featured extensively in DTI Single European Market nationwide promotional poster campaign.
- Supported John Major, the then prime minister, with a speech at the pre-election Wembley rally in April 1992.
- Raised £1 million to establish the Excalibur Scholarship Scheme with the prime minister in April 1993.
- Actively supported New Labour in the run-up to the May 1997 election, and have since been recruited by the government to the Treasury's Industry Team, where I am an adviser to Chancellor Gordon Brown on youth enterprise.

People probably know me best as the founder of Amstrad, which started as a small enterprise and has grown to become an international consumer electronics, telecommunications and computer group. I've sold off some of the company, but remain the major shareholder, chief executive and chairman.

So, why did I decide to become CEO for *The Apprentice*? Because I know what it's like to start from scratch without a mentor. I am a self-made man with my feet firmly on the ground. I enjoy the benefits of becoming an entrepreneurial success, but at heart I am an old-fashioned entrepreneur.

I know my roots and I am proud of them. In spite of some tough times in the press over the years, the public has supported me, and I have both enjoyed success and experienced the challenge of failure through the course of my career.

I can't help the way I am. My East End background might have left me a little rough around the edges, but that's not something I can do anything about. It was a good training for reality; it kept me down to earth and taught me to quickly appraise situations and assess propositions.

I fought my way out of poverty and I remain convinced that others can do likewise too. Society has been good to me. Now the boot is on the other foot and it's my turn to give something back.

I'd now like to introduce you to the other members of the Board – the people who helped me to assess the candidates in *The Apprentice*, Nick Hewer and Margaret Mountford.

Nick Hewer

Nick is one of my most trusted colleagues. Born to Anglo-Irish parents in England, he was educated by Jesuit priests at Clongowes Wood College in County Kildare, made famous by James Joyce in *A Portrait of the Artist as a Young Man*. After a brief stint as a law student, he diverted to the then novel world of public relations.

Over the next 35 years his work took him all over the world as his consultancy acted for such organizations as Amoco, Securicor, Ciga Hotels, Cable & Wireless, Konica and Tottenham Hotspur. He was retained by the Chantilly-based secretariat of His Highness the Aga Khan in France for over 20 years.

In 1983 he was retained to represent Amstrad, and for the next 21 years became an integral part of the company's management, as well as representing me in my many personal and business interests. Responsible for the company's product launches across Europe and North America, Nick set up and coordinated a network of agencies to handle Amstrad's public relations on a worldwide basis. He was deeply involved in my takeover and chairmanship at Tottenham Hotspur, with its attendant court and newspaper battles. In more recent times he has worked with me on my enterprise initiatives with the government. He now lives in France and spends much time travelling: a lifelong passion.

Nick Hewer knows that once I get behind a project, I'll give it 200 per cent. Having been with me since the beginning, Nick knows me very well, and I value him as a sounding board. He is involved mainly in public relations and promotions, but he's been around whenever we've been buying and selling companies. He's a right-hand man when there's a need to discuss the presentation of business figures to the financial community, the need to organize product launches and generally to interface with the media. He's found me a difficult client because I don't like talking to journalists and I don't particularly like giving interviews, but he always persuades me to go along with him in these matters.

Margaret Mountford

Margaret is a lawyer who specializes in corporate law and has an excellent reputation in the City. She was a partner in the top-tier company Herbert Smith until 1999, and has helped me to win a lot of deals over the past 20 years. She's a fiery character and is the kind of person I like to do business with. She has an excellent way of focusing and getting down to the bottom line. She understands that I need to know certain facts, and she's good at categorizing them, then letting me know what they are.

I trust Nick and Margaret's judgement. It's all very well assessing people face to face, but there are practical tasks being set for the candidates and I need to have eyes and ears that I trust watching the candidates every step of the way and reporting back to me.

Ideally, I would love to be a fly on the wall 24 hours a day, but that isn't possible due to my day-to-day commitments. Margaret and Nick have rock-solid integrity – I know they won't mislead me. If I ask them who did a good job when I was out, I am confident of getting an honest and balanced answer.

chapter two

WHAT IS AN ENTREPRENEUR?

What are the main characteristics of an entrepreneur? Are they different from those of a business leader or an effective manager? Of course they are, and I doubt they are skills that can be taught.

Speak to any successful entrepreneur and you will find that few of them had others in their family who shared their drive and hunger to achieve a personal commercial vision, even if they had wholehearted family backing and support. Small businesses are the backbone of the economy in the UK, and the biggest businesses aren't necessarily the most entrepreneurial.

'An entrepreneur –
if there is such a thing
– is a born schemer
who constantly
thinks up new ideas
in an original and
creative way.'

SIR ALAN SUGAR

I'm often asked questions that imply there must be some untold secret about how to become an entrepreneur. They are not questions I like answering because we are all individuals and I don't believe in formulas for success.

Let me see off some of the more common questions before we begin.

Are entrepreneurs and business leaders born or made?

In my view, entrepreneurs are born, but effective business leaders can be made if they are coached well, learn from their mistakes and have the ambition to succeed. However, those who have stayed in the same job all their lives and have reached the age of 40 without doing a deal of some sort, without following an earlier entrepreneurial instinct, are unlikely to suddenly develop entrepreneurial acumen when they hit their mid-life crisis. But who knows? If this sounds like you, and you've got the desire to try, all things are possible – just go for it.

Most of the candidates chosen for the TV series have experience of running their own businesses with greater or lesser success. Aged between 25 and 39, they come from a broad range of backgrounds, including finance, events management, property management, politics, marketing, management consultancy, recruitment, IT, hospitality, sales and communications, and the public sector. Each brings with them a range of skills and experience.

How important are training and education?

Training and education are very important. Education trains the brain (certificates prove that you can think) and training can provide some very important skills, but... theory is no substitute for practice, and, as anyone who spends even the briefest time with me will testify, I do not rate an MBA above high-street experience in business. If you want to learn, if you want training, get out there and do it in the good old school of hard knocks. While you're sitting at home reading a book, the next generation of entrepreneurs will be out there hustling.

The candidates in the show are a very mixed bag academically, although each of them is bright and intelligent. Some are graduates; others left school as soon as they could. A few have professional qualifications, and some have been to business school. I am always interested to see which kind of background provides the most effective survival skills.

Is gender an important factor in becoming successful?

Gender is important in every area of life, but when I am asked this question it usually means 'How do you rate women as leaders?' I'm a great believer and supporter of women in business. Whether someone is male or female means absolutely nothing to me in a business context. Women have been at the helm of some of my most successful business ventures, and Margaret Mountford, a board member on *The Apprentice*, has been one of the most formidable legal players in the commercial scene in London for many years.

The woman at the head of my Hong Kong manufacturing business for many years was so good that she ran rings around most people in the UK. Another female employee, a formidable woman, became CEO of Amstrad France. I also had a woman running the consumer-electronic side of our business in Italy.

In this day and age there is no distinction between the skills of the sexes. An old-fashioned person might expect our engineers to be men – probably dressed in bibs and braces. However, engineers today are as likely to be women – and very talented ones too. The qualities that are needed to become a successful and original entrepreneur have nothing to do with gender and everything to do with hard work and organization – skills that are common to both sexes.

There are tough players of both sexes in the teams on *The Apprentice*, and there have been many surprises as a result. Never make assumptions about gender-specific abilities in business. Nine times out of ten you will be wrong.

Does an entrepreneur need to be a team player?

For an entrepreneur to succeed it is vital that he or she is a team player who can lead from the front while commanding the respect of the team. Entrepreneurs are often mavericks. A maverick is usually an original thinker who may be disruptive and difficult to manage.

A maverick may also be unpredictable and refuse to be part of the pack. Of course it is easier for entrepreneurs to be true to their own style if they are running the organization rather than trying to fit in as employees, but no one is an island and an entrepreneur is no exception. Adapting from being a one-man band to a team leader or business manager can be one of the hardest leaps that a would-be successful entrepreneur will make. Without the help and support of other people, not only among their own team, but also in partnership with other businesses and business advisers, a business loner will not survive.

Operating as part of a team is a tough challenge for many of our candidates in *The Apprentice* because they each want to come across as a natural leader, each wants to shine, and many of them have very clear views as to what will and will not work. I look out for those who can put their own egos to one side for the good of the team and for the good of the overall goal, but can also lead from the front with confidence when required.

Are risk-taking and courage essential to becoming a successful entrepreneur?

Without doubt, risk-taking and courage are prerequisites to succeeding in business, but calculated risk rather than impetuosity or foolhardiness is the thing to aim for. I think of myself as a gambler, but not one driven by addiction. Effective project planning and disciplined time management are essential skills, as is flexibility of approach – this last quality probably being the most important attribute of all.

When several of the candidates combine all the necessary skills I look not just for the best all-rounder, but the one who would fit well into my organization.

So, have you got what it takes?

There are characteristics commonly shared by successful business people and millionaires, so for those who like this sort of thing, I list the recurring attributes below.

Hard work

Self-belief

Planning ahead

Single-minded focus

Tenacity

Organizational skills

Courage

Decisiveness

Action-orientated

Positive thinking

Being ahead of the game

Able to visualize success

Self-discipline

Proactive approach

Regular exercise

Supportive partner or family

Willing to seek advice from experts

Learning from, not dwelling on, mistakes

Gratitude and appreciation

Faith

Adapted from information in The Millionaire Mind, *Thomas J. Stanley (Bantam Books, 2000)*

Don't think for one minute, however, that just by ticking the right boxes you will automatically have what it takes. I can't stress enough that each of us is an individual with our own indefinable creative flair and unique talents that will ultimately dictate whether we have what it takes to sink or swim in business.

chapter three

HOW TO BE AN APPRENTICE

Apprentice – a person who is learning an art or trade either from an employer to whom he or she is bound by a contract or by practical experience under skilled workers.

DICTIONARY DEFINITION

I usually recognize elements of my younger self in each of the candidates who join me on *The Apprentice*. They are all hungry young people and most have already had some experience of running their own show. I want to know whether they have the ability to think like winners, whether they have the stamina to succeed, who can 'lead from the front' and who is more likely to 'hide in the bushes' rather than push themselves forward; whether they are able to enjoy what they do at work whilst maintaining a balance in their leisure hours, and whether they have a proactive vision of the future.

Be hungry

When I first started out, I wasn't interested in making a million, I wasn't thinking about getting a knighthood. It was all about getting some wheels. I wanted a car – and I wanted to be independent. I was also angry, and probably a bit arrogant. I was sick of putting money in other people's pockets when I knew I could earn more on my own. I had seen my father work hard all his life, putting the family first and playing the safe game in order to take care of us. I was at a point when I had no responsibilities – and I knew I didn't have his temperament – I would never be able to stay the course working for someone else. It wasn't a conscious wish to do things differently, but the more I worked for other people, the more I knew I'd rather go it alone.

That was the starting point, and it wasn't an empty, impulsive action. I had money saved up, and in spite of taking what some thought was a foolhardy step, I took it with care. I withdrew £100 of my savings, of which £50 went on wheels (distribution), £8 went on third-party insurance (liability), and the balance of £42 went on stock (investment). I already knew my market (market research) and I knew the main players (purchasing and sales). I had a personal target of £60 per week (business planning), which I aimed to earn by the Wednesday of each week (self-discipline and application). I worked hard to create a place for myself as an effective middleman and deal-maker (negotiation).

It was only after I had been doing my own thing for a while and had the satisfaction of knowing I was making a success of it, that I began to think seriously about exploiting new opportunities – of speculating with new product development. That company, launched in 1967, rose to be valued at £1.2 billion in the mid 1980s.

Overnight success? There's no such thing. Hard graft, self-discipline and the hunger to succeed are the keys.

Personal vision – *Clarify your goal*

Having a vision is about using your imagination, it is about stretching your brain to think differently. It's about training yourself to focus on where it is you want to go, what it is you want to achieve.

A vision is important because if you can't see yourself living your life differently, if you can't envisage a world where your product, your service, your idea is necessary for others' business success, then you don't know where you are headed. It would be like going on holiday without a destination and no road map. You will get somewhere – anywhere – and you might enjoy the view, but you don't know where you are, so you can never tell others how to find the location, and you can never go back there.

Having goals is vital because they are the stepping-stones to achieving your vision. Without goals your vision remains a dream. That's obvious, you might say, but it is amazing how many businesses fail because they don't know where they are in the marketplace; they haven't got a business plan and they are not monitoring their progress.

All sorts of statistics declare that a large percentage of businesses fail within the first 1–3 years of starting up. It is hard to be accurate about this, but look at these examples: in 2002 some 91 per cent of businesses registered for VAT in that year were still in business 12 months later; 64 per cent of those registered for VAT in 1998 were still in business three years later. It's an easy thing to write down, but a harder thing to live through. These figures mean that at least 36 per cent of those people who started up in 1998 did not succeed in the longer term. Their vision and goals were not focused enough to help them survive.

There is a high level of self-belief and self-motivation amongst the candidates who apply to be *The Apprentice*. I have confidence that each of these young people has the energy and wisdom to succeed in business.

TAKE ACTION

☞ If you are thinking about setting up your own business, choose something that you love and have experience in. Map it out: find out what you know, and ask others about the things you don't know.

☞ Don't worry about making mistakes because it is from mistakes that most people learn.

☞ Be bold. Set a target date and a series of goals.

☞ If you're thinking about it, do it! There are no free lunches out there. You can only achieve your ambition by giving it a try.

Desire – *Understand what or who inspires you*

The desire to succeed needs to come from deep within – it's not something you can fake. You need to know yourself and be aware of who your role models and mentors are. Who do you admire? Whose success would you like to emulate? You need to realize what you are trying to get away from, as well as what you want to move towards.

Perhaps you've got your vision, mapped out an immaculate business plan and set your goals. Are you raring to go, or are you feeling stuck? Desire is what you need to set you off on the path to becoming an entrepreneur.

The word 'entrepreneur' winds me up because so many people claim to be one, but very few really are. You can't learn to be an entrepreneur. It's something that is in you. You can learn to play the piano and knock out a few nice tunes, but you'll never be a Mozart; you can learn to paint a house and it will look very smart, but you're never going to be a Van Gogh. In the same way, an MBA on its own won't make you a success in business; a business plan won't guarantee motivation or achievement of your goals. The idea on its own is not enough.

> *'Don't be put off by ifs, buts and maybes in business. There's no such thing as can't.'*
> Tim Campbell

What makes you tick? Are you motivated by the idea of making money or the idea you are planning to launch?

Two kinds of people run big companies: those who started the business and have a major shareholding, and those who just have a job. Their mindsets are quite different. The first has the business at heart and is permanently focused on it performing as it is meant to. Salary is not a big concern; the real reward is a successful company. The second type, the 'jobbers', are more interested in what they get out of it. Once established, they tend to look after number one, covering their backsides when anything goes wrong. They care about themselves, but do they truly care about the business? Have they got the desire that would drive them to be successful entrepreneurs in their own right?

It is important to me that the winning Apprentice has the overall good of my businesses in mind: not to their own detriment, but with a true understanding of 'the business of business'. I would say to all business people that it is valuable to keep abreast of who's who and who has achieved what in business, and to keep up with the business news.

TAKE ACTION

- Ask yourself who your positive role models or mentors are. Do you have any?
- Look at qualities you admire in others who have achieved their goals.
- What is really pushing you forward at this moment? Is it a positive or negative reason? Both can be motivating, but is it enough to make you really crave success?

Drive – *Maintain your own momentum*

Anyone who watched the Athens Olympics in 2004 would have been struck by the sheer hunger and focus of those athletes determined to win against very stiff odds. Nowhere was this more obvious than in the running events. The athletes who won gold medals knew their form and pace. They had trained hard, they had the desire to win, but they also had the drive to succeed. They had planned the race; they had studied the form of the competition; they had trained – very, very hard – so they understood their personal strengths and what they could deliver. That meant knowing when to push and, crucially, knowing when not to push, in order to get ahead. The athletes who tried to accelerate when their bodies were already performing at optimum speed came in second, third or nowhere at all. The ones who had pushed at the right point and stayed focused on maintaining their momentum were the ones who powered over the finish line.

There is great similarity between the mental discipline required to train for sporting success and that needed to make it in business. There is no way that you will consistently beat the rest of the pack without training and without building up your skills. You need to think big but start small.

To succeed in business you need drive, energy, determination, hunger – and you also need the discipline to stay focused, to build your momentum and to maintain a steady pace. There are those who think that running your own business means an easier life. Far from it. When everyone else is clocking off at 5 p.m. you'll still be working. But you will learn your pace; you will learn that coming to a complete halt makes it far harder to start up again.

Doing a deal is like a sprint, but building a business is more like a marathon. And just like a marathon runner, it is better to build gradually and aim to maintain a steady pace than to crash and burn.

There are many enthusiastic, would-be entrepreneurs out there who promise too much, too soon. In the first flush of new business development they make hundreds of calls, they promise the earth to all and sundry, they have such a large range of credit and payment arrangements that customers have to remind them what the current terms of business are. Planning goes out of the window. Contact is either feast or famine. This stop–start approach does no one any favours. Clients don't know what to expect; they don't know what the business is offering, or whether it is reliable. There's nothing wrong with the level of drive that this person has; the problem is that he or she is not building and maintaining momentum. There's nothing wrong with being flexible – in fact it's essential – but don't let others pull your strings. Stay proactive and keep that entrepreneurial start-up energy flourishing.

Sell anything, anywhere. Don't be particular if someone wants to buy – sell to them. But only make deals that you can deliver on. Be conscious that you are developing your client base with every call you make. Keep your cool and play to your strengths. Plan ahead. Be clear about what you are offering, and keep an open mind for new opportunities.

Set your pace and keep in training. When you're going for gold there's no room for self-indulgence. It can be hard for some of the candidates to see how this applies to them because there are time constraints applied to each task. But, in business, time management is important, so time constraints are not the point. The point is that first impressions count and relationships matter. I watch the candidates to assess how each one might conduct him or herself in business.

TAKE ACTION

- Set personal targets and seek to surpass them.
- Know your working pace. Plan ahead to make maximum use of your day, and to ensure you start focused and maintain momentum.
- Stay focused and avoid developing self-indulgent habits during the working day. A pattern of late starts, long lunches and late-night working all hand the advantage to your competitors.
- Be aware of your time and use it to its optimum.
- Make sure you are in control, even when you feel as if you're not.

Capacity for hard work – *Can you deal with adversity?*

There are those who work hard, and there are those who think they work hard. There are also those who work very, very hard for a very long time, but don't recognize the progress they have made, so they quit just before the winning post.

Have you got staying power when times are hard? When you think back over your life to date, did success or material goods come easily to you at school, at home, in your social life? When has your endurance been tested, and how did you react? If you're faced with adversity, do you avoid the problem or procrastinate, or – even worse – do you lose your cool or blame others? Can you keep working when everything seems stacked against you?

I've never been the wining-and-dining type myself. I think it's a waste of time. If you're the sort of person who thinks a hard day's work starts at 11 a.m. with a cappuccino in a café and finishes at 3 p.m. after a long lunch, then (depending on who you had lunch with, of course) you're unlikely to make it as a successful entrepreneur. You're probably either employed by someone else or have a large private income. Wake up! The dot.com boom is long over. Investors are unlikely to invest in pipe dreams any more.

People who have a chance of success in business are those who know what it's like to have their backs against the wall and still come out on top with their integrity intact. They are the ones who have a competitive edge, for whom winning – against all odds – is everything; they listen, dream

'**I'm a man who makes up his own mind. It's what I've done all my life.**'
SIR ALAN SUGAR

large and plan with care; they are not afraid to ask questions, are dogged in their determination, and have no qualms about reinventing the system. They are not necessarily the high-fliers who get all the plaudits; they are the ones who know what's going on at ground level, the ones who chip their way up the ladder, cannily, steadily, one step at a time. They are the ones who will be determined to solve a problem rather than give up.

Make no mistake – there is no such thing as luck in business – just hard graft and keeping your antennae tuned to changes in the marketplace. There have been winers and diners as well as grafters amongst the candidates for *The Apprentice*. I want to find out what each of them is truly made of when they have a tight deadline and have to knuckle down to the task in hand.

TAKE ACTION

- Watch your attitude. Do you think you are owed something by your employer; by your family; by society? If so, think again. Get out there and start creating your own opportunities if you want to succeed in your own right.

- Don't give up, no matter how hard you've been trying. If you believe in something, it is worth continuing with it – not blindly and not without taking stock of your progress to date – but if you've asked yourself the tough questions (see pages 52–4) and you believe you have an original and marketable idea, keep going (after taking professional advice, if necessary).

- Don't expect overnight success. You can strike lucky if you have the right product in the marketplace at the right time and at the right price, but true success takes years and a lot of trial and error.

- You feel like quitting? Keep on trying – just one more time...

Think like a winner

I come from a working-class family. We lived in a council flat in Hackney, east London. In my neighbourhood it was generally accepted that when you left school you went straight to the local garment factory. I had earned myself a reputation as someone who could broker a good deal and who had a talent for selling, so I found myself on a slightly different path – in consumer retail goods.

I learnt early on that it paid to think big and think smart. In my early role, as a salesman selling tape recorders, it dawned on me that rather than selling my heart out for a single-unit order, I could earn much more for the same (or possibly less) effort if I targeted the chief buyer at Currys and aimed for larger orders of, say, 1000 units.

I looked for the big deals and I landed some sizeable orders, but my success at selling was never reflected in my payslip. Instead, my boss penalized me for the special discounts he had to give the larger customers as a result of my orders – even though I was increasing his bottom line. I lost my temper and walked out of that job. Something similar happened in my next job: again I saw red and walked out. Those bosses did me a favour. Had they not been so ungrateful, and had I not got mad, I might still be working for one of them today. Instead, they reinforced my belief in myself and made me determine that one day I would work for myself.

To be a successful business entrepreneur, you need more than just a competitive edge. You need a hide like a rhino, the ability to operate way outside normal comfort zones, a willingness to reinvent the rules, and total, utter, complete self-belief – against all odds.

Self-belief is a critical skill for success in business. Although they have different ways of expressing it, self-belief is a trait shared by all the candidates in *The Apprentice*.

Self-belief – *If you don't believe you can, why should anyone else?*

Do you believe in yourself? Do you know that you have what it takes to succeed? Or are there seeds of doubt? If you naturally defer to others, apologize for your success or don't really believe you can make it, then it won't matter how much financial backing you have, it won't matter how good your product is and it won't matter how much others believe in you. You are your own number one obstacle, and you need to change your attitude – fast!

> '*Look at what you've achieved in life and be confident that you made it possible.*'
> Tim Campbell

It may seem an obvious thing to say, but an entrepreneur needs more backbone than most. You are trying to develop a new concept, but no one else shares your vision; you are trying to deliver to your customers, but the supplier lets you down at the last minute; you are trying to get stock into your nationwide outlets, and your distributor goes bankrupt; you have set up a press launch for a ground-breaking new product line, and the technology lets you down.

When you're running your own show, the buck stops with you – no one else. You are the product, you are the service, you are the reason for failure. It gets up close and personal. And it can hurt – if you take it personally. This is a lesson that some of the candidates find quite hard.

In reality, we all learn from our mistakes – and our failures. The fact is that you cannot succeed if you don't try, and you can't learn without making mistakes. The larger the failure, the bigger the lesson, and the closer you are to success next time. Perfectionism can be a big barrier to progress because it can provoke feelings of failure and hopelessness. Much better to look at what you got right, and to adjust the rest.

Entrepreneurs often have a reputation for being difficult, for ignoring the reasons why not, and listening only to the 'can do' response. That's because a true entrepreneur will aim to overcome all odds. Look at James Dyson. He's been quoted as saying that success is made up of 99 per cent failure. The ones who succeed are the ones who say, 'OK, I'll give it another go. I don't care what anyone thinks.' Perhaps we'd still be living by gaslight if Edison or Swan had given up at the first sign of 'failure' when they were designing their prototypes for the light bulb!

There is a sales-training truism that you have to speak to 20 people who say 'no' for every one who says 'yes'. Why are sales people so often upbeat and positive? Because they welcome the nos if it means they are getting closer to the yes. The trick is to try and convert the initial no into a yes – and fast – so that you cover more ground. And that needs a fast brain, guts and determination.

I'm not saying you shouldn't listen to feedback from your own business advisers and colleagues – especially if you respect the view of those delivering it – but be your own person.

No one else is living your vision, no one else has your drive, no one else knows what is going through your mind – and no one else knows what you are made of.

Unless the person who is offering the advice has enjoyed years of success and is basing that advice on knowledge and experience, have the guts to trust your instincts – provided you've put your basic business building blocks in place (see pages 136–7).

TAKE ACTION

☛ Watch your response to failure. If you are taking setbacks personally, or taking failure out on others, or drinking, smoking or eating too much as a way of coping, give yourself a talking-to and re-focus on your goal. Take stock of the business plan and review what's going on in the marketplace. When you've figured out what you've been doing wrong, adjust it and try again.

- Take action; don't take refuge in self-pity. If you start feeling sorry for yourself, your competitors will gain the advantage without doing a thing.
- Modesty may be an admirable quality, but not when it comes to business. If you're selling your services or promoting a product, your clients want to be able to believe in what you're offering them. Make sure you come across as a safe bet.
- If you have a problem with self-confidence, hide your fear. Feeling nervous and uncertain in new situations is normal. You'll soon adapt.

The will to win – *Do you have the desire to succeed?*

There's no doubt that if you don't care about winning, you probably won't win – not in the long run anyway. To succeed you need a competitive edge.

In many ways my approach to business is similar to my approach to sport. I play tennis. I will never be a brilliant player, but I can serve a good match. I enjoy it because it combines keeping fit with exercising the mind. It is fast, fun and strategic.

When I first began playing tennis I would deliberately choose to play people who were better than me. I wanted to challenge myself to win, to learn, to become the best I could be as fast as I could. Now that I can play reasonably well I also enjoy competing against people who are the same level, or perhaps not as good as me, because it allows me to hone my game, to practise my skills in a controlled way.

Tennis offers interesting parallels with my business experiences.

> '*Teamwork is critical to success. United we win, divided we fall.*'
> Tim Campbell

As the new kid on the block, I had to prove myself, and move fast to cope with the might and weight of the big-boy retailers on the high street. Now, as I no longer have to prove myself, my company can take time when developing a new product, testing it against what we know from past experience and, while still putting ourselves ahead of the game, we no longer need to take such a high-risk strategy in order to improve.

Each candidate takes part in *The Apprentice* to win – they each have the will to win. The greatest challenge is learning how to balance the needs of the team with their own goals and desires – but most eventually learn that the individual cannot succeed alone. The combined talents and success of the team is crucial to overall and continued success.

TAKE ACTION
- How much do you care about winning? Do you keep challenging yourself to learn better techniques? Make sure you are not being complacent. To succeed you need to stay ahead of the game.
- Which is more important to you, personal recognition or the bottom line? Providing excellent service or making a profit? It is admirable to want to help others and understandable that you would like to be noticed, but unless you're running a service industry, gaining plaudits won't pay the bills.
- Visualize what it is like to win – and enjoy the feeling. Winning comes with its own pressures and responsibilities. If being a winner is outside your personal comfort zone, you'll be better off remaining someone else's employee.

Originality and creativity – *Staying ahead of the 'me toos'*

In my business it is crucial to be original, to stay ahead of the rest of the marketplace. If you're manufacturing a mass-market electronic product, i.e. producing the cheapest product with the most features, which will be attractive to the most people, you are competing mainly on margin. In spite of your original features, you can be sure that eventually someone will find a way to copy it.

Apparently, copying is the highest form of flattery. I don't know about that, but I call the result a 'me too' product. 'Me too' products are created by companies that don't have the imagination to break new ground, or that have a 'safety first' policy: following rather than leading the marketplace. Once the 'me toos' start selling my products, I start thinking about what comes next.

Complacency is the death-knell of a company because the market is always changing, trends are always changing, and your competitors are always changing. Never be complacent. Just because something sold well last week doesn't mean that it will next week. If the 'me toos' are on to my idea, then the market is on the move.

Experience of a market is invaluable because you start to understand what sells and what doesn't, and you can begin to assess more easily what will work and what won't – but with that comes another danger: making assumptions.

Never make assumptions – even about something you think you already know. Always ask the marketplace, always test your product, always make sure that your margin is enough to make a profit and that you're selling to a niche that can afford to buy at your price.

Several of the tasks I set for the candidates include elements of creativity and originality. I want to see how they think, how market savvy they are and whether they have the nous to ask available experts for help and advice. Few of them have worked in a creative environment before and it is an area fraught with challenges.

In my companies I am the creative hub. I generate the majority of new ideas. This is both a strength and a weakness. It is a strength because the City and the markets have learnt to trust that there is an awful lot we do right; it is a weakness because if I were to disappear tomorrow, the creative future of the company would be at risk. It is something I am very conscious of and that we're looking to address right now. That's why, in a mature company, choosing the new generation of staff is so important.

- ☞ Are you an original thinker or do you build on or copy other people's ideas? Start testing your ideas on those you trust or on the marketplace – will they fly?

- ☞ Do you imagine the future as a place that is more exciting and innovative than it is now? You've got the right attitude. Are you nostalgic for the past? Use your nostalgia to find ideas that will work in the present, otherwise you may not have the flexibility to survive in the modern world.

- ☞ Don't feel threatened by the competition. Stay awake to what is going on in the marketplace, but don't panic and start copying when you get cold feet. Stay ahead of the pack.

- ☞ Never forget that the customer is always right. This means making sure you can sell your ideas well enough that they are not questioned, and being willing to listen to what people say. Sometimes innovators and entrepreneurs are so far ahead that others need time to catch up.

Imagination and thinking big – *Visualize living the dream*

People ask me whether I started out with a vision of being a multi-millionaire. But that is the wrong question. What's so important about becoming a multi-millionaire?

There are many thousands of successful entrepreneurs and business people who will never be multi-millionaires. Does that mean they are not successful? Does that mean they are not thinking big? Far from it. They are the backbone of the economy and each one is a success in their own right. If all you are looking for is lifestyle, you need to head for a business sector that pays well or make sure you inherit some wealth. There are no personal guarantees via the entrepreneurial route.

My interpretation of thinking big is rooted in business and sales. Thinking big means thinking strategically and planning the optimum deal. The optimum deal is not necessarily the largest or biggest, and is unlikely to be the lowest risk. Thinking big means looking to shift your product, or to supply your service to the biggest marketplace possible. That's where creativity and imagination come in because you need to look constantly at how to reach your market in a new way. For example, cable television is making increasing use of US-style shopping channels, as candidates in the first series found out.

Make sure you know who the big players are in your market sector and that you have a convincing reason why they should want to do business with you.

My imagination and creativity remain focused on the marketplace – what it wants, what it needs and how we might deliver it. Get that right and the rest will follow.

Anyone who knows me or has read my newspaper columns over the years will know I have very little patience with profit and deals made out of thin air (perhaps that should be hot air). During the dot.com boom of the 1990s, millions of dollars were made and lost on the stock exchange on the back of great ideas that weren't founded on substance. These investors and companies were thinking big all right, but at what long-term cost to themselves and the economy? I'm a great believer in building success on solid foundations that will last – and that will serve your family, your community and, by implication, your country and future generations.

Imagination and visualization are important because you need to believe you can succeed – but make sure your feet are on the business ground because, to my knowledge, Walter Mitty (the fictional character who lived in a fantasy world) never made it big.

TAKE ACTION

☛ **Be ambitious and keep your dreams real. Rein in the impulse to act on your lifestyle fantasies until you have the right financial foundation stones in place.**

☛ **Remember that all success starts by selling the right product or**

service to the right section of the marketplace. If you don't know what your market wants, don't guess – ask.

☛ When you are doing deals, don't just think about the short-term gain; think strategically about the long-term big picture. Is this deal taking you where you want to go? I don't mean being fussy about who you sell to, but make sure you know who the big players are in your field and where the money is going to come from.

Business savvy – *Thinking on your feet and reinventing the rules*

If you can get hold of a big brand product and cut the price, you will sell shed-loads. It is quite another ball game to introduce an unknown brand. It takes lateral thinking and a lot of determination to re-create the marketplace and to convince every potential purchaser not just that 'I want one of those' but that 'I genuinely need one of those.'

And make no mistake – you are a brand, in the same way that your product or your service is a brand.

If you are on a limited budget and you need to shift stock or get noticed fast, there is no substitute for personal contact. Retail selling? Get to the most senior decision-maker as fast as you can. Direct selling? Don't be passive – be active – get on the phone, seek out face-to-face meetings, get a sale there and then, and leave your customer with an incentive to get others to buy too.

Stymied by bureaucracy or the way things are 'always done'? Frustrated and hampered by 'the rules'? Then be determined to reinvent the methodology. I'm not proposing all-out anarchy here. Bucking the system won't get you anywhere. You have to work within it to begin with. But industries, like businesses, get stuck

> *'I think there is a false perception in business that you have to be quite harsh ... but there is room for many different and individual styles.'*
> Tim Campbell

in a rut, and if something is not getting through because the system is in the way, the system may be outdated.

Don't waste your time with blockers and jobs-worths, but don't alienate them either because they will just become more entrenched in their attitudes. Use them to get to where you need to be. You may have to operate outside your comfort zone, but take appropriate action to make sure you are dealing with decision-makers at the right level to get things achieved; and please note – this does not necessarily mean the person at the top.

There are shelf-loads of books on successful sales techniques, and directories full of training courses on how to open and close a deal. I will not go into the detail of that here – although if you watch *The Apprentice* you will pick up a lot of practical insight. The point is, you need to stay sharp, you need to stay focused, you need to remember that whatever your sector, profit is the bottom line. The candidates who succeed never forget that they are here to win – that they have to keep thinking on their feet and keep on selling – because there is a team of competitors on their tails just dying to see them get fired!

Think survival. It's a jungle out there, and you need to know that you have the skills to survive if you are lost and starving; and that others want, need and depend upon you to survive.

TAKE ACTION

- Understand your client base. Ask questions. Find out about the structure and size of the company, and, if necessary, check their credit rating. You need to make sure they can pay you.
- Make sure you know who you are talking to, what their role is within the organization, who they report to and whether they are able to make decisions.
- There are jobs-worths and action blockers in every organization, and sometimes they have very charming faces. If you're not getting the result you need, find out who you should be talking to and deal with

them instead. Note: the person at the top is not necessarily the decision-maker for your product or service; they too can be a blocker if they don't understand the value of what you're offering.

☞ Remember that you've got a business to run. By all means do people favours, but not at the expense of your own or your employer's profit or survival. (That is especially true if you have employees or a team reporting to you.)

Flexibility — *The willingness to learn from others and keep an open mind*

Flexibility is the key to survival in business. It is crucial to stay flexible because things change: trends, markets, technology — everything changes, and so do we. I change because I am still learning. I learn new skills every day; I learn things, good and bad, from everyone I meet. Learning is what keeps us flexible, keeps creativity alive; it is what links generations together and allows us to survive.

Change also means that the marketplace will want something from you tomorrow that is different from the product or service you are providing today. It is up to you to find a way of providing it — profitably.

The language of the modern world is different from the language that I grew up with. The vocabulary has changed, and the business processes are different too. On the one hand, business is more formal — a handshake is no

'I don't like liars;
I don't like cheats;
I don't like bullshitters;
I don't like schmooz-
ers; I don't like
arse-lickers.'
SIR ALAN SUGAR

longer enough to secure a firm deal; on the other hand, everything is more large-scale and fast-moving.

Each of the candidates is forced to be flexible in order to survive. They are tested to their limits in the various scenarios and business situations that are set for them in the tasks of *The Apprentice*. Many cite flexibility as one of the most crucial business skills that they have learnt.

TAKE ACTION

- **Make sure you are not being rigid in your approach. Having fixed ideas about how things should be done and completely overruling your team's objections is no way to run a business. If you're being rigid, you're not listening. If you're not listening, you won't survive.**
- **Be aware of what the rest of your market is doing: note changes in pricing, distribution, product features, fashion, lifestyle – and make sure you are ahead in your game.**
- **Know your weaknesses as well as your strengths, and instead of being defensive about them, bring on board others who can help you achieve your endgame. Adapting is the key to survival.**

Millionaire mentality – *Respect the bottom line*

You don't have to be a millionaire to adopt a millionaire mentality, but without it you're unlikely to become one. I didn't start life with the aim of becoming a millionaire. I became self-employed in order to be in control of my own destiny and because I could see a way to make more money than if I stayed working as an employee. Millionaires are financially aware: they are aware of the value of their time, of the fact that margin is more important than cash-in-hand at the end of the day.

Entrepreneurs who start a business must do so with a personal payday in mind. By that I mean that you are in business to make money and you must always charge appropriately for your product, your service and your time. In a start-up business, however, the owner may not expect to pay himself a salary in the first year because all profits are channelled back into the business to help it to grow. A

'Buy cheap, sell high!'
Tim Campbell

personal payday is important because it is a sign that you are being financially astute – and the business is making a profit.

It is difficult to take money out of the business when you want to safeguard the future well-being of the company. If you can channel it back into the business, you will reap dividends further down the line. I have no problem with spending millions on merchandise, plant and equipment, but I can't bear waste.

I can't stress enough how important it is not to borrow money if you can avoid it – and certainly not at start-up stage. Planning is essential, but too much time spent on honing a theoretical business plan and not enough on selling will simply stymie development.

So often there is too much focus on the financial theory and not enough energy going into growing the business. In the early days of growth, any kind of loan can leave your business vulnerable. It is one of the ironies of the business world that if a company owes £50,000 because it has overstretched itself, the bank will have no hesitation in foreclosing on the loan, selling the company assets to get back £40,000 and writing off £10,000. But if you owe £100 million, it is a different ball game – it becomes a matter for the financial advisers, who are able to represent the bottom line in a way that will attract new investors to the failing business. One thing is certain: advisers will never let you down when there is a fat fee involved.

So I keep a close eye on the bottom line at all times. Margin is king as far as I am concerned. I invest profits wisely, and I safeguard the future wealth of my family and associates by keeping the speculative side of my business separate from a more safe and secure property portfolio.

This is one of the key elements that interests me when appraising the performance of the candidates. Will they remember what they are trying to achieve? Is profit, or service, or quality the true driver? Design and catering tasks (see pages 150–60) are particularly interesting for this.

TAKE ACTION

- Are you living beyond your means? There is nothing wrong with aspiring to a better lifestyle, but if you're spending money that you don't have, your profits will be feeding the bank's profit margins, not your own.
- 'Buy low, sell high' is the first rule of business, especially when creating a new product and establishing your profit margins.
- Never forget what your time is worth to your business, and don't squander it.

Have the stamina for success

I have worked hard from the day I took my first job until the present. Call it a work ethic if you like – instilled from an early age by a family that worked very, very hard. I know that I could be a workaholic, but fortunately my family would never stand for that, and the electronic revolution means that it is now possible to stay in touch with the international markets without having to sit by the telephone at three o'clock in the morning.

To be successful you need to have stamina, you need to be physically and mentally fit, you need to be able to cope with immense levels of pressure without losing your cool – and you need to be rigorously well-disciplined. I believe in leading by example, and if I'm not driven and well organized myself, how can I expect my staff to be?

For me, Monday to Friday means intensive work. I work flat out from the time I arrive at the office until the time I go home. In fact, I suffer a kind of guilt sometimes, a ridiculous guilt, if for some reason I find myself returning home earlier than usual. I'll stalk and storm around the house until about seven o'clock, when my body clock tells me, 'All right – you're at home now'. It's the guilt of not being at work. However, I also believe in the importance of family and achieving a balance. Weekends have always been my own. It's the time when I rest. It's the time when I have the human equivalent of a 5000-mile service, if you like. If I'm feeling relaxed and healthy in mind and body when I start work on Monday morning, I can cope with whatever the week throws at me.

The candidates need all their stamina over the intensive 12 weeks that they are working on my tasks. They are eating, drinking, talking, waking and sleeping *The Apprentice*. Stamina plays a key part in their survival. One candidate acknowledged that just because she could work through until three in the morning with no problem, it did not mean that others could, and that she needed to take account of the needs of the rest of the team in order for them all to perform at optimum capacity.

Focus and discipline – *Success needs your personal commitment*

I am a highly disciplined person. My time has value, and I calculate what that value is. Therefore it is critical that I spend my time focused on those things that are the best use of my time and deliver the most effective results.

Anything that is not the best use of my time I delegate. The ability to delegate effectively and to work in partnership with others in business is important in getting the job done both effectively and efficiently. It is a skill that some of the candidates have to learn the hard way.

One of the problems among those people, especially young people, who believe they want to go into business on their own is that they have a vision of a life of freedom and luxury – of living life at the top with all the nice things that go with it. They see themselves sitting behind a desk with their feet up, dishing out instructions. The hard lesson is that they're totally and absolutely wrong. If being in charge of an empire is the motivation for going it alone, you'll be doing it for the wrong reasons because it's not like that at all. In fact, you work much, much harder for yourself than you do for anybody else; and it takes time to get to the top.

Success needs your personal commitment – to keep your eye on the game when the going gets tough; to recognize that you have staff whose livelihood depends upon your success. And once you're successful, to be aware that the economy may be affected by your changes in direction, or poor judgement on the part of senior management.

☛ Take a good, hard look at your strengths and weaknesses. If your weaknesses include putting things off, doing things late, sitting in front of the television instead of getting on with other priorities, you'll have to work pretty hard to take control of your time and change those lazy habits in order to succeed.

☛ If you're the kind of person who is always on the go, always has a project in hand and has an energy and a buzz, you're starting out with the right attitude. The question is, are you focusing your energies on your business niche?

☛ The flip side of this is achieving a balance. There is no point in driving yourself into the ground. If you always have a mountain of paper on your desk at the end of the day and find others are always delegating to you instead of the other way around, you need to assert yourself more and focus on planning. Better planning means you can delegate more effectively and make optimum use of your day (see pages 83–5 and 87–9).

Negotiation skills – *Deal outside your comfort zone in order to win*

Negotiating is really a part of selling – and selling is part of everyday life. It is about winning, about projecting the positive side of your nature, and it is also about taking control, about holding your nerve beyond the point of normal comfort when you want to achieve something. But comfort zones can change depending upon what you are negotiating. There are things we are comfortable negotiating for – the price of a second-hand car, for example; and things that may cause embarrassment or awkwardness, such as negotiating a reduction in dental charges or your gas bill.

If you want something desperately enough, you will go to the wall for it – and in reality everything is up for negotiation. Interestingly, though, not everyone is willing to try or even to succeed. They

> *'There is always room to negotiate!'*
> Tim Campbell

get uncomfortable when the person they are negotiating with gets tetchy; they take a 'no' at face value and won't work at turning it around; they will apologize before asking deeper questions, and look obviously uncomfortable at being forthright. People like that should not be in sales – and if they are would-be entrepreneurs, they had better get a good salesperson on their team to counter-balance their reticence to have even the slightest chance of succeeding.

Good negotiation may take patience, it may take pushiness, but most of all it takes personality and intuition – to know when to push for the hard sell and when to hold back, not to appear too anxious, to wait, and wait and wait ... interminably sometimes ... for the phone call that says you have clinched the deal. As long as the person you are speaking to does, on some level, want to buy, a negotiation is always possible.

Those who are less likely to succeed in selling are the ones who are too polite or too embarrassed to ask the straight questions, who haven't got the tenacity to keep beating away the obstacles. They may close the deals – eventually – but the odds of success are reduced and they are less likely to make high margins. Selling and negotiating are at the root of all the tasks set for the candidates. They need to learn how to adjust personal style, depending upon the market sector they are pitching to.

TAKE ACTION

- ☛ **Do you enjoy the buzz of a good deal? Look at what makes you stop negotiating, and push yourself to be even tougher. The more you stretch the boundaries of your personal comfort zone, the more successful you will be.**
- ☛ **Realize that everything you do in life, from discussing who should do the washing-up to finding out whether the person you are attracted to will go out with you, is potentially a negotiation.**

- Learn to read body language, and see what it takes to close a deal when a discussion drags on and on to no avail.
- Next time you're faced with a 'no' in business, do what it takes to convert it to a 'yes', even if you are inwardly cringing with discomfort. The triumph of success will cure you forever.

Persistence – *Have the tenacity to keep going against all odds*

Persistence implies overcoming obstacles, and you will have gathered by now that I am a believer in the value of learning from the school of hard knocks. Difficulty and adversity really can make you stronger if you have the grit to keep on trying. All success comes from learning. And to learn you need to begin by trying, and trying usually means making mistakes – lots of them.

In my experience, all the successes in my businesses evolved from learning what not to do. You learn what not to do because you tried it once before and it didn't work. You also learn when you are knocked back hard that you are made of sterner stuff than you realized – and that not only can you survive, but also that you are stronger as a result. Not all the candidates can stay to the end of the 12-week job interview process, but I am confident that each of them will have learnt new skills.

To keep going against all odds you've got to love what you do, you need to be fairly pig-headed in your determination, and you need to be very, very honest with yourself.

To keep yourself motivated when things go wrong, you need to analyse where things went wrong. You have to be very realistic. Don't try to blame the rest of the world. The blame lies only with you. Recognize that immediately. You also need a contingency plan.

If a particular project has gone wrong and you can see the reasons why, it might be a case of giving it up forever, or it might be a case of developing your idea differently, or revisiting the costs. While operating on gut instinct may be fine as far as product development is concerned, at Amstrad we learnt early on not to be tempted to let our enthusiasm take over and lead us into the common mistake of making or buying too much stock before selling even one unit. These days we might take a bit of a punt to begin with, but in general we don't get it wrong any more. We're more careful now.

Persistence is a critical skill in business. There is no such thing as overnight success. We're all in it for the long game, and that takes strategic planning and determination to succeed. If you haven't got those characteristics, stick to the day job.

TAKE ACTION

- ☛ **Don't be a quitter and don't blame others. Take stock, then knuckle down and get on with the job.**
- ☛ **Single-minded determination feeds self-belief and will help you eventually to win through. Break the obstacle down into composite pieces and tackle them one step at a time.**
- ☛ **You can be sure that whatever obstacles you are facing, others have faced similar things and have come through them, and you will face much bigger obstacles in the future. Recognize what is in your control and do something about it. Recognize what is outside your control and work around it.**

Hunger for the next challenge — *Enjoy turning opportunities into realities*

I am often asked when I will stop, at what point I will step away from what I have created, saying 'Enough is enough'. The truth is that I can't envisage such a time. I can't imagine not being excited by the buzz of the next opportunity and not having the enthusiasm to develop the idea. One of the things I value most about the culture created in my companies is the energy that is present. We are able to move fast when we have an idea, we can make things happen, we can influence the marketplace (provided we have done our research). There is a hunger for the new and a dread of stagnation, of standing in one place, or letting others overtake us. The hunger is linked to the will to win, but it is also linked to a love of the task and of the industry that we're in.

True leadership is energetic and enthusiastic – it makes things happen. It is what enables you to bounce back after a string of defeats, rejuvenated by a good night's sleep and say, 'OK, bring on the next challenge'.

Sticking with it and being enthusiastic can be tough. It is interesting at what point certain of the candidates show signs of giv-

> '**Many people would argue that the buying of things is the key to their business ... whether you're buying 1 or 1,000 it doesn't mean you shouldn't negotiate.**'
> **SIR ALAN SUGAR**

ing up – perhaps the prospect of working for me is too daunting! Sometimes the process of filming and being apart from friends and family takes its toll. When you are working hard to make your dream business successful, you may not have as much contact with – and time to spend with – family and friends as you would like; dividing your time or feeling alone can affect your performance. Just as the candidates find this a difficult aspect of making a TV series and completing the tasks, it is also a difficult aspect of leading a team in business.

Losing your hunger for your work needn't threaten your future, provided you are not running your own show. If you are running your own show, and there are others depending on you, you need to keep that hunger and energy alive, or hand over the creative reins to someone else who is still buzzing at the idea of doing something new. Hunger is the characteristic that will enable you to overcome obstacles, to think laterally to solve problems and to believe you have the ability to succeed.

A hunger for the next challenge is a key characteristic in those with entrepreneurial personalities: they are always seeing possibilities where no one else can see them. If you have that hunger in you, do all you can to nurture it in either your business or your personal life. It is a gift that will keep you searching, growing and learning.

TAKE ACTION

- Love what you do and do what you love, otherwise you will become unhappy and self-defeating.
- If you enjoy what you do, don't be afraid of expressing your enthusiasm. Enjoyment is infectious and you will bring others along with you.
- A product that has the heart of the team in it is likely to be a better product; it will be more in tune with the market's requirements and it will perform ahead of the competition.
- Recognize your own entrepreneurial spirit and make sure you feed yourself new challenges.

Courage – *Have the guts to succeed*

Success isn't just about being good enough – it's about taking a chance, taking a gamble, seeing an opportunity and having the guts to go for it – to enter into uncharted territory. It can also mean forcing others to sit up and pay attention, rather than accepting their nos at face value.

In Amstrad's early days we were battling to get the retail giant Comet to take our amplifiers. I could not persuade them to take stock, so I had to find something that Gerry Mason, Comet's then marketing director, wanted so that I could gain bargaining power. They needed Garrard record players at increased discount. I managed to secure a deal. Gerry was delighted, and although I still didn't get an order, I won a listing in the Comet adverts that were seen nationally by the public.

Then came the main chance: I encouraged friends and family around the UK to place orders for the amplifiers – and finally, the call came. Comet had received orders for seven of our amplifiers and would therefore take 10 to be on the safe side. I blew a carefully calculated gasket. I knew how they operated. Ten amplifiers meant no repeat orders or roll-out to the main stores. I told them, 'You're Comet! You're not taking an order for 10 units; you've got to take at least 100 or it's ridiculous.'

Since then, we've never looked back, and the relationship between Comet and Amstrad flourished. Some would say I conned them. In fact, I helped them to make a highly lucrative decision.

You'll never be successful if you're cautious. That's why accountants are accountants, engineers are engineers, lawyers are lawyers. The engineer who distracts himself into becoming a businessman is less likely to succeed. He is a different animal. However, nothing is written in stone. If there were rules that we could all follow, there would be lots more multi-millionaires out there in the world. One of the characteristics I like most about the candidates is their courage. Their courage in coming on the show, their courage in taking on whatever tasks are thrown at them, and most of all their courage in facing me – the man with a reputation for being blunt and brutal – and the prospect of being fired, in spite of their best efforts.

TAKE ACTION
- ☛ If you've got an idea you believe in, come up with a strategy to sell it, whether to your corporate bosses, to your marketplace or to another company. Nothing will happen to move your idea ahead unless you are behind it 200 per cent.
- ☛ Play the game. If you have spotted a market niche for your product

and you can't persuade the buyers to take it, find something else that they do want and use that as a bargaining point to achieve your true objective.

☞ Test yourself at every opportunity. Feeling shy about talking to someone influential? Decide what you need to say and just say it. Uncertain about how the marketplace operates? Find someone who does know and ask questions. Need to shift some stock? Get out into the market and sell face to face, or look into bulk selling via other means.

Lead from the front

Leading from the front is easiest if you surround yourself with a team of people who share your beliefs and values and whom you can trust. This is easier to achieve in the early days of starting up a company than later on when the corporation is larg-

'I have never been afraid to "step up to the plate" in business.'
Tim Campbell

er. Once you begin to delegate the task of recruitment to others in the organization, there is no longer any guarantee that you will get to know the individuals concerned. In order to lead it is critical that you are seen, and that your staff know you are not only present, but also that you are interested in – and make it your business to know – what is going on.

You have the vision. It is up to you to communicate that vision to your team clearly and concisely, in a manner that is understood; to delegate effectively and to ensure that you follow through in such a way that individuals take responsibility for their own actions; and to keep it that way. It looks so easy written on the page, but for many people leadership and management are the most difficult areas of running a business. These sections are intended to give you some insight into the way I approach my role.

Leadership – *Self-management and the importance of being yourself*

A leader needs others to follow in order to achieve an objective. That's what a leader is for. A good leader is not necessarily always the most well-liked person in the company, but the best ones are liked because they are respected for their clarity and vision.

Leaders tend to be born rather than made, although it's true to say that some people grow into a leadership role later on in their

> *'I didn't come here to dodge responsibility.'*
> Tim Campbell

careers. Effective leadership is about earning respect, and it's also about personality and charisma. If you want to be everyone's best friend, it will be hard for you to make it in business.

Inspiring others is important, but if you're leading from the front, you also need to inspire yourself, and to inspire yourself you need to understand what motivates you to succeed. That is quite a challenge for the candidates, as each is a follower one day and a leader the next.

In my case it is easy. I am motivated by making a profit, the buzz of the deal and an enthusiasm for innovation – being first in the marketplace with a life-changing product. My personal style is well known. I am upfront, belligerent if necessary, with high expectations, and I do my best to lead by example. My style is also inclusive, however, and I am a great believer in making sure that everyone knows what is going on, and that credit is given where it is due.

In order to gain respect you need to be true to yourself. There is no point in trying to be brutal if it's not in your nature; there is no point in trying to be suave and sophisticated if it doesn't come naturally. In business, as in life, people like to know who they are dealing with. No one trusts a faker.

In business, as in friendships, there is a getting-to-know-you process. Focus first on achieving a successful outcome from the business task in hand, and the liking may follow – as a bonus.

TAKE ACTION

- ☞ Pay attention to the sections on communication and delegation (pages 81–3 and 87–9), the two foundation stones upon which good leadership and management are based.
- ☞ Don't try to be something you're not – but at the same time be sure to work on those skills that undermine your ability to earn respect from your team.

- Be particular about who you employ, making sure they can be trusted and that they will suit the personality of the organization.
- Plan ahead and be disciplined in your approach to self-management. It is hard to earn the respect of others if you do not practise what you preach.

Planning and adapting – *Organizing the organization*

There's no point in asking an entrepreneur what he plans to do next, or whether he visualizes achieving a certain level of success by a certain date. It's like asking a songwriter, 'At what point did you decide you were going to write your next song?' It doesn't work like that. It just happens. It's a natural desire to go ahead and do something else, to move on.

Once you've succeeded in achieving one goal, you go on and do other things, mainly product-orientated. It's simply that once you get on a roll, you're on a roll, and you just keep on rolling. You go with the momentum. You don't just stop.

I've always broken the rules, especially within Amstrad, and we really don't have the conventional corporate structure that you would find in many large companies. I personally feel that if you were to ask every fund manager who has ever invested in Amstrad what bothers them about the company, it would not be whether I am going to do something silly and lose all their money. Their concern is more likely to be that I am the company: 'What happens if Sugar gets run over by a bus?' The fact is that Amstrad won't impose a structure because we want to retain the flexibility to communicate fast and act quickly.

Project planning is important, but it's also important not to become so caught up in your own business plan that you don't act, or stick to the plan so rigidly that you don't adapt.

Each industry has its own rhythm, its own pattern, its own market expectations. The big difference between the tasks set for the candidates and what I do in the real world, is timing. We're open for business all day, every day, all year round. There's no set timeframe for action.

Planning a product as far as I'm concerned is a continual process.

I do not pre-set targets that state we must launch one product a week, or we must launch one product a month. We might not bring out a new product for two years, or we might bring five out in one year. We react to the way the market is moving and what the market needs. Everything we do is market-driven, and in the case of my companies, it's all technology-driven. Rather than bring out a new model of a product for the sake of it, we keep on selling – we sell it to the death. There's no time limit on anything. As long as the market wants it, they'll keep getting it and we'll keep on marketing it.

If a product is doing very well, our aim becomes to enhance the margin. Typically, in the electronics industry, something that starts off costing a certain amount to produce will come down in price when the second lot is made. If your product is selling well at the price you launched it at, then by all means put the additional margin in your pocket. If it's not, think about rejuvenating the market for the product by dropping the price. Even though you're changing the price, there should still be the scope to increase your margin. This applies to selling a service too. Perceived value is important. Make sure you are not underselling yourself.

My aim has been to retain the quick-fire energy and ability to adapt that allows small start-up companies to succeed, while combining it with large-scale manufacturing capability.

There is a small, central, creative hub headed by me. The rest is to do with project management and product delivery. To impose management structure would be to slow down a working method that has its own shape and influence. I have seen too many entrepreneurial companies flattened by jargon and bureaucracy, so I was determined, following flotation, that that would not be the outcome with Amstrad.

- Assess whether your own decision-making system is effective or whether you need some additional expertise on board.
- Be aware of your management style. How do you organize, plan and make changes? Do you want regular, structured meetings, or will the team operate more creatively and effectively without being hamstrung by bureaucratic structures?
- Focus on designing and delivering the products effectively. In my view everything else is peripheral to that and can be sorted out as and when necessary.
- Be extremely organized where finance is concerned, make sure you are not under- or over-pricing your product or services, and ensure you have excellent advisers.

Focusing on finance – *Never borrow what you can't repay*

I never had any money when I was starting out. My business was always run on what I could finance myself. Now, as then, profits are ploughed into the business as soon as they are made, which allows me to do more. Now, of course I use the facility of the bank's over-draft, but I always treat it as a fallback. Overdrafts are for certain times of the year when you are building up stocks and inventory – you need help to finance that – but it's short-term finance because you see it quickly turn back into the black. It's vitally important in my view not to get third-party finance. Being lean forces you to stretch yourself. It focuses you. It keeps your eye on the ball.

I subscribe to the train of thought that says: if you want finance, what are you going to put up to the bank? Why should the bank take a risk on you? There are no free lunches in this world. It doesn't help to moan about banks and financial institutions that you think should be in awe of your business plan. The chances are that the only one in awe of your business plan is you. Why should they give you any money? They don't owe you anything. If you don't have collateral and you haven't proved yourself in the market yet, you are a risk – to yourself as well as to the financial institutions.

So, start small. Start with a limited amount of your own finance. When you start to make profits, and when you can show a healthy balance sheet – after two or three years – then you might get the bank's attention; then you might get a financier's attention. But if you're looking for someone to finance you in the short term, you'd better see your mum or your uncle or (and I don't recommend this one) rob a bank. No one else is going to give it to you. It is no use trying to run, in financial terms, before you can walk. People want to be big, they want to be successful; they think of an idea on Monday and they want it to happen by Friday. But, unfortunately, life doesn't work that way.

There's nothing wrong with being optimistic about your plans and outwardly buoyant, so long as you are personally counting the beans. By all means try to stimulate enthusiasm and be positive, but to be successful you have to remain down-to-earth and realistic yourself.

Each of the tasks set for the candidates involves a budgetary element. How they spend their seed money contributes to their overall success.

TAKE ACTION

- ☞ Work within what you have financially – not within what you would like to have.
- ☞ Do plan your budget, but don't expect any large-scale investments from a third-party financier until you have proved yourself to be a safe bet.
- ☞ Start small and grow; it will allow you to develop more solidly and learn from your experience rather than your mistakes.
- ☞ Make sure you are on good financial terms with your suppliers and retailers at all times, but maintain the possibility of being flexible if their goods or the discount structures become prohibitively expensive.

Communication skills – *How to communicate your ideas*

Communication is critical to the efficient running of a successful company. It's vital to convey information quickly and effectively. It is an obvious thing to say, but it's important that everyone knows:

- **What is going to happen.**
- **When it's going to happen.**
- **Why it's happening.**
- **Who is responsible for making it happen.**
- **What the expected outcome will be.**

The message needs to be concise, precise and to the point. Get the facts out, don't cloud the issue, and don't try to be too clever. Get the points across – and look at the person you're talking to. If they still look a bit confused, go down a level in your explanation – especially if you're starting to bombard them with technicalities.

I am the kind of person who keeps on the move, so I do speak to a lot of my staff every day. But some employees work off-site or in another time zone, so I make it my policy to keep in touch by email: brief, concise and to the point.

I have no patience with those who claim not to know what is going on, and I have no respect for managers and leaders who do not communicate properly. We are surrounded by Star Wars' technology that allows easy communication anywhere, any time and with anybody.

Speaking to people face to face is usually the preferred and most effective method of communication, but that is not always possible or realistic. Phone calls are more personal than email, but impractical on a large-scale basis and potentially time-consuming. Meetings have their own agenda.

There are far too many rules bandied about regarding how to conduct meetings. Most of them are utter nonsense. You cannot generalize about the size or frequency of meetings. They are as large

> *'Making and keeping good relationships in business is key.'*
> Tim Campbell

or as small as they need to be. Sometimes there are only one or two people present; sometimes there are 30. If we're briefing a whole team of people about a new product, or finding out the progress of something that involves 15 people, they all need to be there.

Communication, leadership and project management go hand in hand. You can't simply communicate your ideas once and expect everyone to act on them in unison. Communication is about keeping in touch – with your staff, with the marketplace, with your external suppliers – and it is about all parties taking responsibility for keeping each other informed.

Just as one of the challenges of running a creative business is to judge the right moment to launch a new idea, so too is it important to decide when to invest in new communication technology. There are those among my staff, and some cheeky journalists with long memories, who will remember that back in 1993 I made a statement during the filming of a BBC television documentary to the effect that my staff would not be using email. These days that may seem absurd, but at the time it was the right call. There was no point in my businesses using email if the rest of the world was still sending faxes and telexes to communicate with each other. The commercial world depends upon precise information changing hands fast, and by proven reliable methods. Email was a risk at the time.

The good news is that Internet technology is now used extensively around the world and I am able to communicate from a central point to everywhere and everybody that I deal with.

TAKE ACTION

☞ If you've got something to say, say it. Don't compose a lengthy memo that is word perfect but that no one will read. Communicate concisely, effectively and promptly in order to transmit your idea.

- ☞ Don't censor information unless it is highly confidential. Your team will be much more cooperative if they feel included in what is going on.
- ☞ Keeping people informed is not the same as giving each person a say in the decision-making process. Keep your door open to feedback, but make it clear who is the decision-maker for the task.
- ☞ If you are leading a project, don't rely on a single communication to get the job done. Combine the written with the personal and make sure all parties know what they are meant to achieve and by when.

Managing time – *How to make maximum use of your most valuable resource*

My motto is: 'Always clear your desk every day.' I never leave any paperwork on my desk at the end of the day because doing so means that something is being put off, that a decision is being delayed. It is an ethos that I try to instil in the rest of my team. I become very frustrated if things aren't done when I expect them to be.

Do not put off messages, answers and decisions – they've got to be dealt with one day. It's a bit like your gas bill or electricity bill. You leave it hanging around, but you know you've got to pay it, so you might as well pay it immediately. That's my philosophy. Bang – in comes a question from a member of my staff. Bang – there goes the answer back straight away. Obviously that can't be done on every occasion, but I try. It's a kind of discipline.

It annoys me tremendously when people I deal with do not follow the same policy: not prioritizing in the correct order, not getting things done, putting off decisions, thinking that they'll get around to it another time. The thing that irritates me the most is having to ask people why they haven't done something and listening to the excuse, 'Well, I was going to do it tomorrow.' It's a response that doesn't go down very well with me when I want an answer now – and I always want things done now!

Of course, you can't apply this philosophy to everything – but it's the sense of urgency, the use of time that is important.

Time is the biggest asset I have in respect to interfacing with the outside world as well. As far as international business is concerned, dealing with America or the Far East, for example, I could easily be at work 24 hours per day. In running my business, it is part of my job to 'keep the plates spinning' so that other people can get on with their work too. I have to provide the people in the Far East with enough information for their 8 a.m. start so they can get on with the job and will be able to give me answers later in the day. It's no good leaving them up in the air, because there's a time difference that could potentially be costly when the rest of their world is closed.

The same applies to staff in the UK offices. The person at the top needs to be ahead of the game, blazing the trail for the next action, the next strategic move. I guess you could say that I keep everybody on their toes.

Time management is possibly the greatest challenge for the candidates because each of the tasks is tightly time-bound. There are no extensions possible. This forces some tight and creative solutions, and enables some candidates to break free of previous slower-moving habits of decision-making.

TAKE ACTION

- ☛ Time management is linked to self-discipline and needs a robust approach to both planning and delegation. It's a valuable commodity, and planning your time will help you to be more focused and help clarify priorities.
- ☛ Be rigorous in your approach to your 'in' tray, and be clear as to your own core skills. Be aware if you are doing a job that could be done just as effectively (albeit not in quite the same way) by someone else.
- ☛ Avoid self-indulgence. Don't get distracted by personal emails, and if possible make sure all emails are screened by a third party so you see only the essentials.

- Learn to delegate (see pages 87–9). You may need to take time out to train someone, not once, not twice, but six or 10 times. However, once they understand your requirements, you will become twice as effective and they will have learnt a new skill.

Motivational style — *Inspiring your team to deliver and to succeed*

Motivation is all about inspiring people. Your team may consist of just you and one other person, but there is probably a whole host of other people in the supply chain who may or may not feel part of what is going on, and may or may not feel appreciated.

Sometimes the people you need to inspire are remote from the centre of decision-making, so they might not feel the same sense of 'ownership' of the project as its main creators. Designers, engineers and manufacturers are often divorced from the final result, and consequently also divorced from the final success of the project.

I will sometimes use my time to explain to these vital partici-pants in the process: 'Do you realize that you are working on something here that is far superior to anything else in the market-place? And if my gut feeling is right, when it gets out there, it's going to be a winner, and when you walk down the high street with your children at the weekend, you'll look in that shop and you'll say, "I made that, you know, I'm a part of that." Or "I made the software", or

'At the end of the day we're looking for someone who is going to come and work for me ... There's a certain sort of Sugar culture.'

SIR ALAN SUGAR

"I designed it", "I drew it", "I actually manufactured it", "I loaded it on a lorry", "I delivered it" ...' I think it's very important that people such as software engineers and mechanical engineers, who do specific tasks to make specific parts, are not left in isolation, but understand what they are doing their jobs for.

They also get to hear: 'This product is late because you didn't do this ...' or 'This product is going to be ready because you did do this'. I motivate, but I'm also honest about situations. As candidates get to know each other, they really come to value the ability of their team members to motivate them through the rougher, tougher moments.

TAKE ACTION

- Be aware of how far your team extends – from the receptionist who is the public face of the company to the warehouse operator who needs to deliver stock on time, to the retailer who is handling orders from a multitude of other customers, or, in the case of a smaller operation, to your neighbour who has the kindness to take delivery of a heavy parcel when you are out. Make sure they understand their part in the process and are appreciated.
- Be consistent. Everyone has off-days, but the office is no place to vent your anger in a personal crisis, or take it out on your colleagues if you are not feeling very well.
- Stay positive. Even if you are annoyed, make sure you are focused on the art of the possible and encourage everyone to keep working towards achieving a common goal and a positive outcome.
- Don't humiliate people in front of their colleagues. If you've got something to say, blame them in their professional capacity; don't be tempted to insult the person.
- Stay well-motivated yourself. Make sure you keep your eyes fixed firmly on the goal and do not get distracted by peripherals.

Delegation – *Remember to trust your staff and not do their jobs for them*

The secret of delegation is to make sure you are delegating the right tasks and to follow through on them. If you are the leader of an organization, it is a poor use of your time to do administrative tasks. If you are the engineer, by all means make your suggestions to the marketing department, but don't start writing the advertising copy. If you are the project manager, don't start undermining your team by doing all the work yourself. You get the idea.

Taking on too many staff can be a mistake too. It's important not to over-invest in staff. Only take on new people when you have to. It affects your bottom line, and your overheads add up.

I took on my first employees in the early days so that I didn't have to spend my time packing parcels. Later, other facets of the business, such as doing the accounts, would be delegated. The company then got to a size where the organization of transport was becoming too time-consuming for me, so I had to get someone to do that as well, to leave me with the most important elements.

Delegation, for me, is to do with delegating the physical tasks that need to be performed throughout my business.

With the exception of some products in the audio range, I don't think I have ever delegated the responsibility of dreaming up a product. What I call the key, blockbuster products have all been down to me.

My philosophy is to never ask someone to do something that you can't do yourself. That's not everyone's philosophy, of course – and, importantly, it is not the same as trying to do an expert's job for them. I have enough proficiency in engineering to be able to sit with an engineer and collaborate with him or her. I have a reasonable grasp of what software is capable of doing, although I haven't got a clue how it

> *'Sir Alan manages ... by empowering you to develop your skills from the outset.'*
> Tim Campbell

does it. Software is my biggest challenge because I don't have a true understanding of how long it reasonably takes to create it. I therefore have to remember to keep off the backs of the software designers. In every other aspect of the business I have a great understanding.

If you look at most successful businesses, you will find that the person at the top of the tree has a large portfolio of skills in that particular business.

Time management is dealt with on pages 83–4, and it works in partnership with effective delegation. We have all seen newly appointed managers who have not yet grown into their roles acting 'down' and creating havoc for the tier of staff below them by trying to do their jobs for them. By all means share the benefit of your experience and encourage people on their way, but don't take over. If you do, you'll end up doing everyone's job for them, which means you'll disappear under a mountain of paper with no one left to delegate to – and they may well have to start doing yours.

It is always interesting to see how each of the candidates chooses to delegate and whether they follow through and manage the process effectively.

TAKE ACTION

- ☛ Make sure there is an able person filtering your emails, and if you find it hard to delegate, make sure you choose the kind of person who is not afraid to point that out to you.

- ☛ Follow through on the task, and set time-bound target dates for completion. Delegation is not the same as letting go. It is about managing a task through a third party because your own time is better spent focused elsewhere. It is like having an additional arm, not cutting one off and hoping it will work without your brain to instruct it how to move.

- ☛ Be aware that your task may be delegated further, and make sure that the person who has taken responsibility for that action is also taking full responsibility for the consequences.

- ☛ Don't be tempted to take the task back if it hasn't been done exactly to your specification. Brief the person you have asked to do the task and get them to alter it to your requirements.
- ☛ Be clear and concise, making sure that the person has understood fully, and don't apologize for giving them their job to do.

Valuing change — *The importance of being adaptable*

As Charles Darwin proved over a century ago, we need to adapt in order to survive. Nowhere is this truer than in business.

I started off as a wholesaler and then became a manufacturer. Since working in manufacturing, Amstrad has evolved to take advantage of many changes in technology: developing products that have transformed the hi-fi industry, capitalizing on the CB radio boom, working in partnership to deliver satellite TV to the UK, and it is now at the cutting edge of telecommunications. We intend to survive for many more years yet.

Being adaptable to change applies to creating, selling and marketing a product (there's more about that in Chapter 5). It also applies to project planning and team-working. The reason our company is able to respond quickly to changes in the marketplace is because of our flexibility. Many of the large conglomerates are hide-bound by bureaucracy and it can take an age for them to make a decision. In my companies we are able to move fast, and with the right products are able to gain the market advantage.

When assessing our candidates, I want to be sure that whoever we appoint is flexible in approach, a good listener, quick on the uptake and fast to see and respond to new opportunities.

TAKE ACTION

- ☛ If you're getting too attached to your business plan and your spreadsheets, the chances are you're losing your nerve or are not thinking creatively enough. Plans should be made to explore whether an action can be taken, not as a straitjacket for non-action or prevarication.

- Flexibility implies an ability to listen and to take account of the opinions of others, which means a more rounded, better-informed decision will result. If you find yourself saying 'no' as a knee-jerk response, think again and listen up – you might be told something useful.
- Flexibility is not the same as changing your mind or being indecisive. Flexibility means being open to change if the market requires it, in order to remain profitable and to survive and thrive. Use a flexible approach to make a better decision, not just any decision.

Managing people – *How to know what is really going on*

There are no formal management structures in my companies – much to the disapproval of many. I know what is going on partly because I have told people what to do, and ensured the team is in place to deliver, and partly because I ask what's going on. It's not always easy to implement, but in theory it really is that simple.

I manage people by remaining focused on the task. Delivering the task is the result of clear briefing, effective delegation, time management and getting regular progress reports.

Obviously I am working with people, not robots, and the personal element comes into it too, but the greater the sense of urgency in a business and the more focused the task, the easier it is to maintain control because staff don't have time to be distracted or diverted into non-essential activities.

I'm not saying we haven't had our problems. When the pressure is on, all kinds of behaviours raise their head, but in general I find that direct questions will eventually get me the answers I need.

I am the inspiration in my company. Like it or not, that's the way it is. I manage the show, but I've got a lot of very good people around me who actually implement my plans.

During the 12 weeks of *The Apprentice*, I want to see which of the candidates the rest turns to in times of trouble, and who has the inspiration to lead them to success. Those trouble-shooters are likely to be amongst my finalists, and one of them will be my winner.

TAKE ACTION

- ☛ If you run a large team, make sure you have lieutenants you can trust and who are effective people managers.
- ☛ Ensure that you have briefed everybody fully and that everyone understands his or her role in the process.
- ☛ Use your skills in time management and delegation to ensure that you are getting the feedback you want from the team.
- ☛ Trust your instincts. If you are getting glib answers, or someone is evading a direct question, keep asking questions until you get to the truth.
- ☛ If you have a non-player in your team, find out what the problem is and either move them to a role that will play to their strengths, or help them to leave.

Inspiring loyalty and trust — *Value your staff and they will buy into your vision*

I said at the outset that loyalty and trust are important values in business. The marketplace is a battleground, and unless you go into battle with an army that backs you 100 per cent, you will lose. No matter how brilliant you are at planning, strategy, sales or marketing, you will fail.

I am extremely lucky to still have many of the people who were with me when I started out. My staff tend to stay either for 20 minutes or for 20 years!

Loyalty and trust have to be earned, and that usually takes time. It is earned as a result of delivering on your promises, of saying what you mean, of leading from the front and of being supportive to staff during times of challenge. It is also born of including others in your vision of the future. All successes are a team effort. No one person can achieve all their aims on their own. Therefore the rewards need to be shared.

The challenge for the candidates is to create loyalty among their team-mates and to win the respect and support of the advisers assigned to the task, with no benefit of past history and no time to build a relationship. It is interesting to see how they persuade people to help them achieve their goals and what kind of alliances build up within the teams over time.

TAKE ACTION

- ☞ If you feel you are not respected as a team leader or project manager, and don't have your team's loyalty and trust, take a good hard look at yourself and figure out why. If you can't see it for yourself, ask the team – they'll soon tell you!
- ☞ Be honest with your team. You don't necessarily have to tell them everything that's going on, but be straight and don't fudge difficult issues.
- ☞ Never ask anyone to do something you wouldn't be willing to do yourself.
- ☞ Be willing to take tough decisions and don't hide behind excuses.
- ☞ Be inclusive in your praise as well as your criticism. If it was a team effort, acknowledge it as such – don't keep all the glory for yourself.
- ☞ If insubordination rears its head, find out why it has occurred and nip it in the bud.

Rewarding enterprise – *Recognize success and ensure your staff benefit*

Although I don't believe in heaping praise on people just for doing the job they are paid to do, I fervently believe that people should be rewarded materially for their efforts, recognized for their successes and that long-term loyalty and commitment to the job should offer financial gain.

There are many different ways of rewarding people, and every company is different and has different needs. Personal and team recognition are probably the greatest motivators there are and should never be underestimated.

Of course, within the context of the TV series, the candidates are unable to reward each other materially, but it is interesting to see whether credit is given when it is due for hard work, and where it is given for loyalty and personal support. The personal factor often influences the candidates' decision-making when it comes to electing who not to send to the boardroom for possible elimination from the team – and the chance of the main prize. The supportive team member will often reap the reward for their support by not being selected for the boardroom. I am never impressed by this tactic. In the real world, tough decisions have to be taken for the good of the business.

TAKE ACTION

- ☛ Review your staff's pay scales in much the same way as you would decide how much you could spend on a project. Begin with the margin and work backwards.
- ☛ What can you afford to pay? If the answer is 'not enough', you will have to be creative and offer variables, such as flexi-time or part-time work, more holiday, etc.
- ☛ The more financially secure the company, the more able you are to look at long-term investments that could benefit loyal staff.
- ☛ Although everyone needs a salary cheque, the majority of people work because they enjoy the environment or the job. Never underestimate the power of peers and the effectiveness of being appreciated for a job well done.

Enjoy your life

Although I am guilty of living to work, the person who does not strike a balance and have outside interests as well is a very dull individual. It's true to say in my own case, however, that the boundaries between work and play tend to get blurred. That's why it is so important to enjoy what you do. Without that enjoyment you will lead a very unhappy life.

I have a strong interest in aviation and took up flying in the late 1970s: it's something I do to relax and I really enjoy it. More recently, my business instinct kicked in when I recognized that the market was now ready for an executive air service. So I decided to start up an air charter company specializing in private aviation.

We currently have three large jets and a charter brokerage division, which enables us to extend the service beyond our own planes, so we act as a broker to arrange flights on other companies' planes as well. Why queue up for three hours at Heathrow when you can speed up the process by using a corporate jet? You'll still have to go through the necessary security procedures, but the process is faster and more personal.

The point is that at a relatively low start-up cost I saw a window of opportunity that crossed the work–leisure divide. We started the business in 2003, and it is doing extremely well.

That said, it is not always a good idea to blur the boundaries between work and leisure. What is important is that you enjoy what you do and do what you enjoy. If you're not having fun while you work, you need to think seriously about changing what you are doing.

Enjoying the challenge — *Love what you do and do what you love*

The Amstrad culture is one that exists because of its innovation, because of its fighting spirit and because of its realism in understanding that we have great competitors amongst us. That is the spirit that is in this company, and that has been in this company for over 30 years. If we were to remain in business and offer just what everyone else offers, we would be dead in the water.

We are not a giant organization. We are a small cog in a giant wheel of an industry. We exist by fighting the big boys, and by using the flexibility that we enjoy as a medium-sized company and that the large companies can't have. Lack of speed is their Achilles' heel. Why can't they do things? Because they're slow, they're lethargic. Amstrad is fast. We're on to things quickly. We maintain a quickness, a fast 'in and out' culture.

I am a great believer in sticking to what you know. Had I not liked the electronics industry when I first got into it, I would have got out fast. I like this business. It's fast and it's exciting. You never know what is going to come next, what is going to be developed next.

Anyone in business has to enjoy what they do. I am fortunate that my employees share my enthusiasm for this business — especially the ones who have been with me a long time.

Some years ago someone described what we do as the

'It's all very well ranting on about team, team, team. I'm not going to employ a bloody team. I'm going to employ a person.'
SIR ALAN SUGAR

'Amstrad Effect'. That's a great compliment. I can't remember who said it, but it means bringing out something new, something that changes the world, changes the face of business. That's what I strive to do. That's what Amstrad is about, and it's one of the things I love most about the business.

The candidates who impress me are the ones who have the ability to rise to each challenge; I want to know which of them is actually enjoying the process!

TAKE ACTION

- If you're aiming to be a part of a large organization, ask some hard questions about whether it is the right corporate culture for you. Unless there are good reasons for them, frequent job changes on your CV raise more questions than they answer.

- If you're planning to start or grow your own business, make sure you know why you've chosen the sector you're in and check whether you enjoy what you do. If you're only in it for the financial opportunity, you'd better plan an exit strategy too.

- Understand your niche and where you fit in the marketplace. If you understand the rules of the game, you'll be better placed to win and take up a different position next time.

The bigger picture – *Remember the work–life balance*

I work hard and I play hard. It may sound like a cliché, but it's true. I start my day early and I work flat out. If I happen to find myself at home earlier than usual, I feel uncomfortable. The work ethic runs deep in my veins, and I don't think I'm going to change now.

But I have a family, too, and they are crucial to my happiness and my success. They are also part of my day, and I am a huge believer in the importance of work–life balance. Once I am at home they become my main focus.

The body, unlike a car or a computer, wears out on a daily basis.

It gets tired and it needs sleep. Creativity and originality need rest and nourishment. There's no point in becoming burnt out and dysfunctional because your business and your staff will suffer. The bigger picture is about family, children, friends, community, the world at large – and enjoying and appreciating life.

TAKE ACTION
- You're not a machine, and creativity and confidence can thrive only in a well-rested, well-nourished body. Be as rigorous in the way you manage your personal time as you manage your time at work, and remember to put your loved ones, not your profit margin, centre stage.
- Your mind is fed by a number of different influences, whether the buzz of a football match, the thrill of taking off in an aeroplane or listening to live music. You can only be in touch with what is happening in the marketplace if you are also in touch with the people who live in it. If you are glued to your desk seven days a week, get organized – and get a life!

Personal recognition – *Enjoy celebrating your successes*

I like to win – in business as well as in sport. When you reach a certain level of proficiency in sport, you want to take on people who make you work hard to beat them in order to get better. But in business I don't mind being second, third or fourth because that also means doing very, very well. Sometimes you've got to be realistic. I'm not going to make more computers than IBM or Dell, and I'm not going to make more televisions than Sony – that would be ridiculous because the effort to lead the pack could also drive the company to failure. So if we make the third or fourth largest quantity, or even the tenth or whatever, that's great.

I value the recognition that I have earned because I know how hard I and others in my companies have worked to achieve the level of success that we enjoy today, and I also know how far we have come. I choose not to live the lavish lifestyle, but there is no question that I live comfortably. I definitely find time to enjoy myself, and if I can find a way of doing some business at the same time, I will probably do that too.

Within *The Apprentice*, the treats enjoyed by the winning team at the end of each task are very much part of the incentive to participate – and they are all aiming for the final prize!

Staying the course and facing the threat of the boardroom are hard challenges for the candidates: the promise of final recognition is great, but they are living an artificial life for 12 weeks, cut off from friends and family. It can sometimes be that way in business too – that is why getting on with your colleagues is important and why it is important to remain focused on what you are doing and to remember why you are doing it. I would recommend committing with equal dedication to your 'off-duty' hours, to allow yourself to enjoy your well-earned leisure and maintain a balance, so your loved ones don't suffer.

TAKE ACTION

- ☛ Celebrations are a form of milestone to check how far you have come and where you are in achieving your goals. Take time out to enjoy your successes and to take stock of the position you have reached in the marketplace.
- ☛ Although it's not my style to do so, there is a case in some industries, such as the media, for networking socially with influential colleagues. You will gain recognition and have access to new business opportunities if you know the right people.

Fast forward to the future

It's very important for me to recognize that I am now in my late fifties and what that means for my businesses. One of the things I like about myself is that I realize my weaknesses, and one of my weaknesses is that as I get older I have to learn to understand that there is a different commercial world out there – entirely different from the one I grew up in. It's no longer a world where one trader talks to another and strikes a deal, where you can generally rely upon a level of honesty and integrity whatever the sector. It's now a cut-throat world driven by a new wave of young business people who have been brought up in a different way – a way that doesn't automatically include loyalty as part and parcel of the business equation.

When I talk about loyalties changing, I don't mean company loyalty. I mean in respect to buying and selling, customer and supplier relationship loyalty; 'handshake' loyalty. There's no point me arguing and screaming or shouting about it, wanting things done in the old-fashioned way. I have to adapt. Of course it's very hard for me to adapt because old habits die hard, they really do; but I have to accept that the business world is changing and to learn to understand it in its new guise.

I do this by recognizing the need to employ young people: young lieutenants who are thinking the same way as others in the marketplace, who are brought up in this new world and know how to operate in it.

Be the best – *Desire to achieve your full potential*

There is no point in being half-hearted about doing something. Putting in long working hours at half-speed is a waste of time and will lead to reduced ability to perform effectively and poor results. My personal goal is not to be better than everyone else – that smacks of a superior attitude that I would not respect in anyone. My personal goal is to be true to myself and to become the best that I personally can be.

A desire to be the best is a trait shared by most taking part in *The Apprentice*. The majority show a tremendous level of commitment and are determined to show themselves at their best. That's what makes a lasting impression on clients and customers – and potential employers!

TAKE ACTION

☛ **Only you will know what your goals are and how you see yourself in life. These areas are closely linked to self-belief and self-discipline (see pages 52–4 and 66–7). Much of what you learn and how you react in business will teach you about who you are, but as well as knowing your strengths, try to observe consciously and improve those aspects of your nature that are your weak points. Your business is an expression of yourself, and it will benefit as a result.**

Putting something back – *Contributing to the bigger life picture*

I do charity work not because I want people to say what a good fellow I am, but because I believe it's the right thing to do. There is nothing more satisfying than meeting an unemployed youngster from, say, Glasgow and hearing him say that my speech has inspired him, that he is going to go out there, get stuck in and have a go.

For the last few years I've felt that I want to put something back into the community. I really get a buzz out of helping someone else take the route I've taken and do exactly what I've done. There's nothing wrong, of course, with inheriting wealth or enhancing it and making it better. Lord Kalms, then Stanley Kalms of Dixons, was a classic example. He worked in his father's business and succeeded in taking it from one level to another – a great achievement. I look back to the 'old days' and reflect upon the place where I started, and I think about the people I grew up with and the community I knew, and I want to put something back. I think it's very important to put something back; it cannot just be one-way traffic.

'Belief in what you're doing is important – and making a contribution is important to me.'
Tim Campbell

I am a massive taxpayer in this country. Just to wind myself up, I keep pictures on the wall in my office of cheques written to the Inland Revenue – £48 million in one year, £28 million in another. Some people would go to extreme lengths for the right not to pay that money. Many actually leave the country to avoid paying such amounts of tax. But you know, as far as I'm concerned, I live in this country, I like Britain, I like British people, I have to live by the rules. I have learnt to take a very pragmatic view. I don't look at the £48 million tax I paid – I look at the other £120-odd million that I was allowed to keep.

I'm very much a British person, and I like to support where I've come from. The fact that I earn a significant amount of money gives me choice and allows me to make charitable contributions that will make a difference to a community. My work for charity has nothing to do with my businesses. My businesses are commercial ventures. The money that I invest in charitable concerns is strictly personal.

Belief in what they are doing and a desire to make a difference in life is common to all the candidates. They aren't just involved for financial reward – that is clear.

TAKE ACTION

- Success and financial independence bring responsibilities. You have made it at the expense of and with the help of others, so make sure you are not assuming the glory is all yours. Give credit where it's due.
- We all have roots and we each owe our successes in part to others we have encountered during the course of our lives. Have you thought

about who you should be grateful to, and have you given them due gratitude and recognition?

☞ Putting something back is related to the idea of work–life balance. Take stock of the way you use your time. If you are always 'too busy' to help others, you have got something badly wrong.

☞ Self-regard comes from giving to others. It is a lesson that we often learn too late in life, so I am passing the information on now, for free.

☞ I've said it before in a different context: no man is an island. As a kid, did you ever give yourself an extended address in your exercise book? My House, The Street, Hackney, London, England, UK, Europe, The World, The Universe? We are each a part of something bigger than ourselves, and it's important to remember that.

Keep learning – *To succeed you need to be hungry for new experiences*

Growing up through my own business life I must have had mentors, but don't ask me who they were because I don't know. There would have been, throughout my life, people that I used to pick up snippets of information from. I would have absorbed it, taken it in like a sponge, not realizing at the time that I was learning from someone that I admired, and then later overtook. I've done that, and I've seen it happen many times.

I've reflected back on my life and can think of lots of people who I once looked up to as business idols because they were running a business that had made £100,000 turnover in a year; but then, three years later, I'm running a company with a £3 million turnover and I've overtaken them. That is the way of the world, and there is another generation up and coming that will do the same to me. So there are lots of people I've learnt from, and I hope there are many who have learnt from me. That's what success is all about – learning.

For the rest of my life I'll learn, as will others who've reached the top. That's why many organizations and companies have as their figurehead a man or woman of 60+ years. Not because he or she is an expert in a particular company's business or products, but because they know, they've seen everything, they've tried everything. They've listened to every salesman, every marketing person, every engineer, every production planner. They've absorbed the valleys and mountains of industrial disaster, financial collapse, economic downturn, political change. They've seen it all, so they know what not to do. You can't replace that. You can't get that degree of experience and knowledge out of a can, and you can't buy it in a book. You can't put, corny though it may seem, an old head on young shoulders; the young head is going to have to learn the hard way. So I'm learning all the time – and I am hoping that the winning Apprentice will too.

TAKE ACTION

- Keep an open mind and recognize that every day you are learning something new and that lessons can come from both the most obvious and the most unlikely sources.
- If you think you already know it all, you are likely to fail in business, so if that is your instinct, take stock and start listening. You might be surprised by what you learn.
- Continuing to learn is one of the most important keys to succeeding in business. The business world is constantly changing, so make sure you are willing to learn new skills or you will get stuck in an outdated rut.

chapter four

INTRODUCING THE CANDIDATES

Some people might expect that applying to be my Apprentice would involve the interview from hell. Well, I don't intend it to be hell, but the process is demanding, and it ensures that the person who gets through the process will be good – bloody good!

I give the candidates 12 tasks to perform. These are designed to be tough. They are designed to push personal boundaries and to put each candidate under pressure. They are designed to bring out the true personality of each individual. They are also intended to be realistic – in scope, in timeframe and in results.

The rules of the game

Even in business, where every company is seeking new ways of operating, there are basic rules of engagement. It is important to be trusted; to be seen as someone who is straight – who delivers what's been promised on the date arranged and at the price agreed. To help our ambitious young contenders to stay on the straight and narrow – and to ensure that the odds remain even across the pack – we drew up the following rules.

Rules of all tasks

- Candidates must not misrepresent themselves or make any false claims during the course of the tasks.
- Candidates may not receive assistance from anyone familiar to them who is not part of the task.
- They may not mention *The Apprentice* or Sir Alan Sugar while researching.

The Apprentice is not an ordinary job interview, but the criteria for selection are the same. I want to see who can make brave decisions and have the courage of their convictions; who can come up with creative and flexible solutions; who is likely to pass the buck or cave in under pressure. I want to know which candidates I can rely upon for personal loyalty in a crisis, and which are more interested in personal gain than the success of the group. And I want to know who I could work with: who I would want to see at the helm of one of my companies, representing me, my family, my staff and all that the Amstrad organization stands for.

What I look for in the candidates

The candidates who are short-listed for *The Apprentice* offer an interesting cross-section of skills and abilities, and come from a wide variety of backgrounds. The 12-week interview process, with barely any access to friends and family, is a personal journey for everyone involved in the project.

What it takes to get to the top depends upon where you envisage 'the top' to be. For some it will be running a department, for others it will be running a multi-national organization. Whatever your chosen path, trying to leap from A to Z in one motion will not work. On the other hand, dividing your challenge into business targets and progressing in conscious steps can take you to Mars and back if that's where you want to go.

As for academic qualifications – although they are an increasingly important currency in getting your first job, they are not a true indicator of longer-term commercial success. The lists below show how millionaires of different academic backgrounds ranked, in order of importance, the qualities shared by all millionaires.

'Is there room for more than one true entrepreneur in an organization?'
SIR ALAN SUGAR

NON-ACADEMIC AT SCHOOL	ACADEMIC AT SCHOOL
Being honest	**Having a high IQ**
Getting on with people	Being honest
Self-discipline	Having a supportive spouse
Having a supportive spouse	Having a passion for your work
Having a passion for your work	**Getting on with people**
Seeing business opportunities that others don't see	Seeing business opportunities that others don't see
Being well organized	**Being a specialist**
Finding a profitable market niche	Being well organized
Ignoring unconstructive criticism	Ignoring unconstructive criticism
Having mentors	Having mentors
Being a specialist	**Self-discipline**
Having a high IQ	Finding a profitable market niche

Adapted from information in *The Millionaire Mind*, Thomas J. Stanley (Bantam Books, 2000)

The characteristics marked in bold are interesting, as these are the traits that are placed significantly differently in the two columns. Those with a high IQ seem to think the need for self-discipline is less important than those who are non-academic, and those who consider themselves non-academic seem to reject the importance of IQ altogether. Perhaps the non-academics put 'getting on with people' higher up their list because they don't have a piece of paper or the right background to open doors for them. Similarly, they need to be self-disciplined because they have more to prove. They also rate being a specialist less important, which might mean they are more flexible in approach. These things apart, there are more similarities than differences between the two lists. However, the non-academic list may suggest a greater capacity for hard graft.

The candidates in *The Apprentice* are hand-selected from

thousands of applicants. I take as a given that they are bright people with the kind of commercial background that means they are up for the tasks. I am on the lookout for an intelligent person who can work alone, as well as operate as part of a team, and can think independently in an original way. I want someone with an all-round portfolio of skills, plus strong sales and marketing ability coupled with good organizational abilities.

I do not want someone who expects to learn from a training manual and then implement those lessons. Rather, I am after someone with innovative ideas – who is excited about those ideas and has the energy and commitment to take them forward.

Straightforwardness, honesty and integrity are crucial in my company. If you are working with someone who reneges on a deal or who doesn't deliver, things can get tricky. I don't like it when people don't listen, or when they misinterpret what has been said. When you are in business it is important to conduct yourself in a professional manner and for people to know they can trust what you say. Loyalty is a great thing – a very important quality – but it's hard to judge whether someone has it until you've known him or her a long time. Only when tricky situations arise and circumstances become confrontational do you start to see whether employees have themselves or the company in mind.

Of vital importance is understanding the 'business buzz'. If you don't get a buzz from 'doing the deal', there is no point in starting a business in the first place. Creating something for your own personal satisfaction is a hobby; sharing the experience with friends and a network of other enthusiasts is also a hobby. It only becomes a business when you start to make hard cash.

I need to know that my chosen Apprentice understands what is meant by a profit margin and appreciates the importance of the bottom line. I will be seeing that person's character and ability develop over a long period of time, so I want to pick a jewel that will sit in the crown of one of my businesses.

'I hope that one of the candidates will have that entrepreneurial spirit ... that it will shine through.'

SIR ALAN SUGAR

Board members Nick Hewer and Margaret Mountford know me and my businesses very well. Although each decision about the candidates rests ultimately with me, I need them as my on-screen board members to help me be objective. Each week it is their job to monitor the progress of the two teams of candidates and to report back to me on their findings. Their observations are invaluable. After listening to their accounts of proceedings we give the candidates their opportunity to explain and justify the decisions taken. One team will win; the other will lose.

The losing team will have to face me in the boardroom, and one of the members of that team will be fired. Fourteen candidates are eventually whittled down to only two for the final task. It is quite a journey – and tough at times – but we enjoy every moment of it.

In each series I hope that one of the candidates will have that entrepreneurial spirit – that everyone will see it, that it will shine through. It's not something you can hide or camouflage, and it's not something you can pretend to have either. First impressions count, but it is only as you get to know people over time – their working patterns, how they relate to other people, how they rise to a challenge, whether they deliver what they promise – that you get to know their true worth.

If a business is hunting for an Apprentice, will it want a creative maverick and risk-taker who can come up with new ideas, or a safe pair of hands who can inspire confidence and ensure the company delivers what it has promised on time and to maximum profit? The ideal would be neither of those, but a combination of both.

The Apprentice follows the fortunes of 14 dynamic, determined, business-minded young people, who had the guts to reply to our advert, as they compete to become the person I want to help me run one of my £multi-million companies. I need to make it clear that in my view this is not a game. It is for real.

There is no point in bringing together the skills and talents of a group of people with entrepreneurial spirit, unless they are going to learn something that they can each take away to benefit their own lives.

There may be only one winner in the television series, but each and every candidate has the talent and skill to be a winner in his or her individual business life.

Series 2 candidates

The candidates for our Series 2 apprenticeship are:

Alexa • **Ansell** • **Benedict** • **Jo** • **Karen** • **Mani** • **Michelle** • **Nargis** • **Paul** • **Ruth** • **Samuel** • **Sharon** • **Syed** • **Tuan**

It didn't take long to put aside any comparisons with the first series candidates. This is a completely different group of people, bringing different ideas to the table, and with a different group dynamic. In business, as in life, it takes all sorts, and I knew I would enjoy seeing how this new group coped with the task challenges as I put them through their business paces.

Alexa

Age 27
Management consultant

- **Was MD of a Young Enterprise company while still doing her A levels**
- **BA in Economics**
- **Spent a summer working for an investment bank in New York**
- **Previous fast-track consultant**
- **Captain of her tennis club and runs the London Marathon**

BEST QUALITIES: Energetic and enthusiastic about things. Goes wholeheartedly for anthing she commits herself to. Also values really good friendships and enjoys the company of others.

Ansell

Age 33
National sales manager

- **2 GCSEs**
- **Won a number of key nationwide incentives including 'Top Field Sales Executive – New York at Christmas'**
- **Sales manager for a marketing company**
- **Previously had a short career as a footballer for Millwall**

BEST QUALITIES: Confident, enthusiastic, articulate, good fun and determined.

Benedict

Age 32

Managing director of a consultancy firm

- **Master of Laws**
- **Director, Centre for Law Ethics and Risk in Telemedicine**
- **Member of the Royal Society of Medicine**
- **Previous associate for company undertaking research into the occupational health, safety and welfare of seafarers**

BEST QUALITIES: Very focused, determined, sees things through to completion once he sets his mind to it, however tough. At his best when he has a specific goal in his sights.

Jo

Age 35

Founding director of training company

- **BEng in Manufacturing Engineering and Business Studies**
- **MA in Human Resource Management**
- **Life Coaching Diploma**
- **Also works as a freelance writer**

BEST QUALITIES: Someone who never stops, always on the go, full of life, passionate, energetic, never takes no for an answer, creative, enthusiastic and has an answer for everything. Never gives up and always provides the entertainment.

Karen

Age 33
Lawyer

- **University of Aberdeen Diploma in Legal Practice**
- **Former RAF officer**
- **Worked on the Freedom of Information legislation**
- **Also fully trained as media operations officer**

BEST QUALITIES: Vivacious, confident, intelligent, desperate for a challenge. She's a good friend, a great mother and a fantastic employee. Strong person who is a quick learner and believes in herself.

Mani

Age 38
Management consultant

- **Runs his own business facilitating executive team workshops**
- **Previously set up a speed-dating company that is still running profitably**
- **BSc Physics**
- **PhD research project in Experimental Physics**

BEST QUALITIES: His solidity, balance and sincerity and his sense of humour.

Michelle

Age 25

Programme manager for telecoms company

- HNC in Business Management
- Qualified nail technician
- Worked as a check-out girl at Kwik Save

BEST QUALITIES: Motivated, positive, tenacious, happy and has a good sense of humour.

Nargis

Age 37

Pharmacist and PhD research student

- **Member of the Royal Pharmaceutical Society of Great Britain**
- **Qualified teaching assistant**
- **Worked as locum pharmacist for community, prison and hospital pharmacy**
- **Previous relief manager for national chemist**

BEST QUALITIES: Loyal, good at fighting her own and others' corners, vibrant and liberated, has lots of presence, uninhibited, tenacious, good humoured even in adverse situations, cool headed in heated situations, direct and not afraid to say it how it is.

Paul

Age 26

Recruitment consultant

- **BA Combined Honours: Business & Community Enterprise with Sport, Recreation & Health**
- ***Sunday Express* Young Entrepreneur of the Year award winner**
- **Previous development manager, delivering school and university talks on benefits of taking a gap year**

BEST QUALITIES: Fantastic salesman, fast thinker, very quickly builds rapport with people to all levels, powerful personality, enthusiastic, should be famous for something, centre of attention wherever he is and everyone loves to be in his company.

Ruth

Age 27
Head of operations and sales

- 9 GCSEs
- Previous team manager for a loans company
- Worked as an administration officer for the Department of Social Security
- Also worked as a bar attendant, a steward for a football club and a youth trainee

BEST QUALITIES: Loyal, focused, self-motivated, proud, ambitious.

Samuel

Age 35
Product innovation specialist

- **BEng Manufacturing Engineering**
- **Was a sponsored student gaining hands-on industry experience while doing a 'sandwich degree'**
- **Master in martial arts**

BEST QUALITIES: Determined, passionate, extremely energetic, supremely confident, results-driven, loyal, friendly and fun-loving.

Sharon

Age 30
Business and education consultant

- **BA in Corporate Communication**
- **Chartered Institute of Personnel and Development Postgraduate**
- **Previously worked as a lecturer in Communication and Media**
- **Was a customer assistant for a major supermarket**

BEST QUALITIES: Honest, reliable, trustworthy, compassionate but most of all lots of fun. Has the creativity and determination to get the most out of all aspects of life. Friends say that she is an inspiration as she has done so much in such a short space of time.

Syed

Age 30

Founder of own IT recruitment business

- **BTEC National Business and Finance**
- **Headhunted to become business development manager in the IT recruitment sector**
- **Previously a restaurant and PR manager for the White Starline Group owned by Marco Pierre White**

BEST QUALITIES: Highly motivated, success driven, dynamic, energetic, professional, confident, persuasive, enthusiastic.

Tuan

Age 26

Financial consultant for building society

- **CeMAP (Certificate of Mortgage Advice and Practice)**
- **Worked his way up in the company since the age of 19**
- **Started his own business based on his car hobby**

BEST QUALITIES: Ability to interact with anybody, immensely approachable, insatiable ambition to succeed in life and adaptability to overcome the challenges that face him in the professional or personal arena.

Series 1 candidates

Tim

Age 27
Transport manager

- **11 GCSEs; 3 A-levels**
- **BSc in Psychology**
- **Chartered Institute of Personnel and Development Diploma**

One of the youngest candidates, and inexperienced commercially, but self-disciplined, with an excellent brain and sound business instinct.
Winner of the first series of The Apprentice.

Saira

Age 34
Sales executive

- **4 O-levels; 2 A-levels**
- **BA in Humanities**
- **MA in Environmental Planning**
- **Corporate sales manager for an online recruitment company**

Loud, determined, likeable, energetic and a brilliant saleswoman.
Runner-up in the first series of The Apprentice.

Paul

Age 34

Property developer

- 9 O-levels
- **Basic and advanced sales for an international car dealership**
- **Work and Method Study Certificate**
- **Systems Analysis Certificate**
- **Founder of a lucrative property management company**

A highly effective salesman, with many characteristics that reminded me of myself. Semi-finalist in the first series of *The Apprentice*.
Fired: Task 11 – The interviews

James

Age 34

Investment banker

- 9 O-levels; 3 A-levels
- **BSc (First Class) in Land Management**
- **Member of the Royal Institution of Chartered Surveyors (MRICS)**
- **Securities, Futures and Derivatives Representative (SFDR)**
- **Finalist in *Property Week*'s Young Property Personality of the Year**

An astute project manager with a proven property background. Well liked, and a natural diplomat. Semi-finalist in the first series of *The Apprentice*.
Fired: Task 11 – The interviews

Miriam

Age 26

Hotel manager

- **4 A-levels**
- **BA in French and Spanish**
- **Manager of an exclusive hotel in the French West Indies**
- **Founder of an events management company**

Focused, professional, with a highly personable manner and very effective team player.
Discovered a natural skill as a TV presenter.
Fired: Task 10 – TV selling on a marketing channel

Raj

Age 30

Internet entrepreneur

- **8 GCSEs; 3 A-levels**
- **LLB in Law (upper second)**
- **Founder and managing director of an estate agency**

Personable, astute in business and very able, but too ready to let others take the glory.
Fired: Task 9 – Direct selling of mobile phone service (Tottenham Hotspur)

Ben

Age 29
Headhunter

- **1 GCSE**
- **Certified senior account manager**
- **Awarded Global Consultant of the Year for the largest executive search company in the world**
- **Runs his own headhunting firm**

A big hitter with business grit, leadership ability and negotiation skill, but lacked budgetary experience.

Fired: Task 8 – Maximizing profits at a farmers' market

Sebastian

Age 29
Recent MBA graduate

- **4 A-levels**
- **BSc in Natural Science**
- **Securities Institute Diploma**
- **Registered member of the Financial Services Authority**
- **MBA from INSEAD**
- **Commercial pilot's licence**

Talented, intelligent, personable, and respected as a team player, but never really showed me his true colours during the series.

Fired: Task 7 – Charity auction of celebrity promises

Rachel

Age 32

Charity fundraiser

- **4 A-levels**
- **BA in German**
- **Chartered Institute of Management Advanced Certificate**
- **Fund-raising manager for one of the largest national children's charities**

A talented individual, but her skill set, voluntary sector background and approach to the tasks were inappropriate for my businesses.

Fired: Task 6 – Creating an advertising campaign

Matthew

Age 39

Mature student

- **BA in Business and Computing**
- **Postgraduate Diploma in Marketing**
- **Member of the Institute of Marketing**
- **Self-qualified stockbroker regulated by the Securities and Futures Authority**
- **Conservative parliamentary candidate**

A pleasant, but awkward character, he played his part in the early tasks, was supportive of his team and well liked by all.

Fired: Task 5 – Closing the deal in an art gallery

Adele

Age 29

Retail manager

- **7 GCSEs; 1 A-level**
- **Diploma in Performing Arts**
- **Set up and manages a lucrative property development company**
- **General manager of family firm**

A talented businesswoman, and a gutsy individual who is used to being in control and doing things her way. She found being away from her family difficult, and her defensive manner made team-building a challenge.

Fired: Task 4 – Running a retail department in Harrods

Miranda

Age 26

Estate agent

- **8 GCSEs**
- **BTEC National Diploma in Performing Arts**
- **GNVQ in Leisure and Tourism**
- **Owned a successful mail-order directory company for performing arts professionals**
- **Founder of her own market and exhibitions display company**

Has a proven background in business, and had some good ideas, but never really showed her true potential on the show. Her panic decision to sell stock at less than cost price in the first task was a problem for me.

Fired: Task 3 – Discount buying 10 items

Lindsay

Age 35

Communications manager

- BA in Creative Arts
- Postgraduate Diploma in Broadcast Journalism
- Postgraduate Diploma in Internal Communications Management
- Founder of the UK's first national car-sharing agency
- Finalist for *Cosmopolitan* Women of Achievement Awards
- Internal communications manager for an oil company

Has a track record of achievement in business and took what she thought to be a brave decision to go against the wishes of her team – but it was her downfall, as she wasn't listening to market advice.

Fired: Task 2 – Designing a product

Adenike

Age 30

Restaurant owner

- 9 GCSEs
- BTEC in Business and Finance
- BA in Business Studies
- MA in International Business
- MBA from PACE University, New York
- Owns and manages a top-end restaurant and runs large events for corporate clients

A self-made woman who is used to being in charge. It was hard for her to be a follower instead of a leader.

Fired: Task 1 – Street-selling flowers

chapter five

TESTING THE CANDIDATES

Basic business skills

This section of the book has been written so that you, the reader, can adapt the tasks the candidates undertake by considering the issues discussed and questions raised in the context of your own business circumstances. If you work in business, you will have been in situations where you have had to carry out tasks similar to the candidates' challenges; so use your own experiences of trying to sell, buy, negotiate, or start a business project to learn more about your suitability to succeed as an entrepreneur.

The following skills apply to you, to me, and to anyone who is in business. The best advice I can give you, whether you are starting your own business or have aspirations to progress within your current career environment, is that you need to start progressing from where you are, not from where you'd like to be, or where you think you are.

Be realistic about your level of experience, your level of working capital and your abilities. Don't try to pretend you are someone you are not, but take stock and assess whether you have the skills to succeed. Where there are gaps in your knowledge or experience, find advisers or business partners to help you achieve your aim – but make sure they are people that you know (if only through recommendation) and that you can trust.

TO BE SUCCESSFUL IN BUSINESS YOU NEED TO:
- Understand your strengths and weaknesses.
- Understand the value of time.
- Utilize what you are best at, and focus the optimum amount of your time on doing it.
- Employ or pay other people to do the rest of the tasks.

COMMERCIALLY YOU NEED TO:

- Focus on the bottom line.
- Focus on achieving your target, e.g. profit or sales volume, or numbers of some kind.
- By whatever efforts are necessary, make sure you plan the task successfully.
- Be well organized.
- Be able to grasp a situation quickly.
- Be prepared for disaster.
- Be flexible/adaptable.
- Realize that timing is crucial – ensure you're entering and leaving the marketplace at the right time.
- Build in regular 'reality checks' to make sure you're still focused, profitable and backing the right product.

Each of the tasks set for the Series 1 candidates was designed to test core business skills that are relevant to every business, whether in a service industry, in manufacturing, in commercial or retail sales, and increasingly in the public sector as well. The general comments and guidelines given here are intended to inspire you, to give you food for thought whatever your walk of life.

Whether you are a young entrepreneur, a mature business person, or someone who has had self-employment thrust upon you and you're hungry to launch your own venture, I hope that these tasks will enable you to reconsider your own approach to business and to learn and adapt as necessary. The tasks were designed to assess the following business skills:

Street selling – understanding your market
Product design – innovating versus reinventing an old idea
Discount buying – how to win at negotiating
Retail management – stock selection and sales skills

Closing the deal – focusing on the bottom line
Advertising – marketing and branding
People management – influencing, leading and keeping on track
Margins – controlling your costs
Direct selling – the challenge of selling face to face
Sales presentations – communicating the message
Interviewing – interviews and how to survive them
Project management – the art of planning and leadership

The tasks may change form in each of the series, but these 12 business skills remain at their core.

Watch your mouth

There's one lesson that I have to teach the candidates quite early on. An organization has room for only one big mouth, and you'd better be sure that that big mouth is the person at the top.

If the person at the top loses his or her cool, the person on the receiving end will probably accept it – albeit unwillingly. If the company's lieutenants try it, it doesn't work. If you have a problem, don't lose your temper – get another opinion and make sure you refer the issue upwards. You can be sure that it will eventually get to the top anyway, so you might as well deal with the problem yourself and nip it in the bud.

Remember – business isn't about you: it's about making a profit for the good of the company as a whole. Anything you do to jeopardize that jeopardizes the fortunes of others in the company as well.

Business lessons and tasks

The lessons and tasks outlined in this section follow the progress of the Series 1 candidates as they attempted to put them into practice. Before the candidates knew what awaited them, we divided them into two teams: girls versus boys. The boys chose to give their team clout by naming it 'Impact'. The girls debated long and hard before they came up with 'First Forte': perhaps that's what sowed the seeds of discontent that dogged the girls throughout the early tasks.

For a list showing the order of tasks for our Series 2 candidates turn to the back of the book at page 257 and assess their skills on the chart on page 258. If you can guess which of the candidates ultimately becomes my Apprentice, I'm impressed. Use the 'Fired or Hired' assessment charts on pages 260 and 261 to record their progress.

Business lesson 1: Street selling –
Understanding your market

I am often asked how I decide which business ideas are runners or winners and which to walk away from. The truth is that much of the decision-making comes down to experience. We all make mistakes and learn from them along the way. But the most important business lessons are:

- To truly understand what the end consumer wants.
- To ensure that the product is suitable for the market – by that I mean in price, in quality and in volume.
- To establish that the product has enough potential to be life-changing.

Every product needs to be innovative and offer something new.

The reason I have no interest in 'me too' products is because if they're already on the market, there's no certainty that anyone will buy them from us. An entrepreneur concentrates on keeping ahead of the game.

Getting the market to change

Great business success stories are all about getting the market to change. I'll give you a classic example: Amstrad didn't invent computers, but we recognized that we could make them at a very, very low price. More than that, we made computers that performed in the same way as other computers. In that way we expanded the home computer market.

Before the advent of our low-priced, IBM-compatible computer, computers were used only by business people and accountants and were very expensive items. Amstrad changed the world – quite literally, we changed it. We brought out the IBM-compatible computer for

£400. No one could believe the price. The other computers on the market were all priced in the region of £4000. We changed the market forever because we were producing a life-changing product. We had a similar success when we brought out word processors at a cheap price while everyone was still using typewriters. The mobile phone is another example of a product that has changed everybody's lives. We're not taking the credit for that, obviously, but as we develop new products in this marketplace, we hope that they will expand the market horizons too.

I confine ideas for expansion to things I am genuinely interested in, and ensure that I have rock-solid customer knowledge – of what they will buy and what they want – before I begin the expensive process of product development.

The art of selling

Selling is really a simpler task than buying, provided of course that you have the right product to sell. At the end of the day the right product will sell itself for you. Once your market knows it's out there, they will seek it out.

Of course, you can't sell something to people that they don't want. You can try – and people do try – but if you do, you don't end up with customers for very long, and you definitely won't get a repeat purchase.

In our industry we're always talking to the same customers. We don't have anyone else to sell to! So we need to take responsibility for maintaining our side of the relationship. There's a balance to be achieved between not lumbering them with too much stock while getting them to buy as much as possible.

In the electronics market it's a false economy to oversupply customers beyond the level that the market will take because it ties up the retailers' cash, it takes up their shelf space and it leaves a bad taste. They will remember it as a bad deal.

The same may not be true in other industries, however. If you were a jeweller in the West End of London, you might decide to offload stock in bulk because the customer could be a transient buyer you are unlikely to see again. That might be an instance where heavy, forceful salesmanship could be used to great effect because you're not anticipating repeat business. However, a provincial jeweller might be less likely to take such a tough stance because he relies upon selling to a smaller nucleus of people and wants to build a reputation of good service and good value.

The fashion industry offers a great example of a sector where high-pressure selling can bring results but turn people off longer term. Most people will, at some time, have gone into a clothing store where a retailer is putting on the pressure to such a degree that you end up buying something that you don't want just to get them off your back. But one thing's for sure – you won't go back there again. You'll never go back, even if you see something nice, because you don't want to be intimidated into buying something else that you don't want.

Repeat business

Repeat business is vitally important for the profit and longevity of a company. You must not risk alienating your customers if you want them to come back again. An intuitive understanding of body language is crucial. You've got to be tough but reasonable, and you've got to understand who you're selling to.

Planning your approach

Selling a product is all about recognizing your objective, then planning and acting to achieve the right result. There are no statistics to help with the sale of a new or innovative product, so you have to be ready to impress customers in other ways – through investment.

What attracts customers?

- Features.
- Price – it needs to fall within their range of disposable income.
- Facilities.
- Newness/originality.
- The 'everyone should have one' factor.
- It should be an easy buy, a worry-free purchase.

What attracts traders?
Traders don't tend to be innovators. They want:

- A safe bet, an easy sell – preferably with a track record.
- Statistics to show them how, when and where to sell.
- Investment to help them market and sell the product.

Spotting a niche

One of the characteristics of successful business people is their ability to spot a niche opportunity in the marketplace and to grow it into something bigger. My own break into manufacturing was through recognition of a very small market for an accessory (a polythene hi-fi cover) that manufacturers were then producing using a process that was rather expensive – simply because they didn't wish to invest in machinery that would enable them to be made far more cheaply. I recognized that I could make them at a much lower price if I made an investment in the right machine.

It was quite a gamble at the time because the market wasn't huge, but it was growing. I could make the covers at about a quarter of the price that the other people could make them for. The clever thing was that I could sell them at a slightly lower price but in the same price range as the others were selling them. I had a massive margin, whereas they didn't have much of a margin at all.

The sales personality

No matter how well organized you are and no matter how many features your new niche product has, you will only make a success of your business if you can sell. The salesperson needs to have personality, drive, a competitive edge, focus and the ability to close the deal. It was these characteristics that I was looking for in setting the first task for the candidates.

Task 1: The hard sell

CHALLENGE: **To earn the greatest profit by street-selling a perishable commodity.**

AIM: **To buy cheap, sell high and maximize profit.**

RULES AND REGULATIONS

☞ The teams are given £400 seed money to start their own one-day business.

☞ They can use only seed money for the specific task or money earned directly from the specific task.

☞ They have to buy stock and sundries for their business. This involves negotiating the best deal possible on whatever they think will sell.

☞ Teams can sell only in specified locations.

☞ The teams have a few hours to sell as much as they can.

☞ Teams cannot try to sell their product within 30 metres of an existing stall or seller selling the same product.

☞ The teams have to reconcile their receipts and sales.

☞ The winner is the team that makes the most profit.

SKILLS TESTED

☞ Being street smart.

☞ Buying stock at the cheapest price possible.

☞ Selling at the optimum price.

☞ Selecting a location where they can close sales effectively.

☞ Recognizing whether or not their strategy is working and to adjust a) location or b) price, as necessary.

☞ Not dropping the price too early in the day.

☞ Selling in large numbers by working hard and closing sales.

Location, location, location

In this context being street smart means knowing the city well enough to choose locations where there will be enough passing traffic to allow the possibility of bulk sales, and where the type of customer is likely to part company with hard-earned cash.

Flexibility in choosing both location and price is necessary, depending upon the type of product for sale and whether or not it is perishable. There is usually quite a bit of debate among our candidates on this point. Some know their locations better than others.

Right customer, right price

Perishable products command different prices depending on the time of day and location. Punters at the Wimbledon tennis championships, for example, will buy strawberries at a high price at any time of day, no matter what size the portion (although quality of presentation is an expectation). However, people buying the same quality of strawberries from a street market will pay less towards the end of the day because the market-traders have to drop the price if they want to clear their stalls and avoid wastage. And goods like flowers, which the Series 1 candidates had to sell, have an even greater range of prices, places and customers.

Crucially, this is also a test of team-building, leadership, professional skills and honesty. At this stage in the programme it is not about individuals within each team competing with one another; it is about working together to keep out of the boardroom and avoid being fired. The team that realizes this first and pulls together is more likely to succeed.

The first task is always a challenge for the new and first-time leaders to rein in all the egos. Once the strategy is in place, will all the team members agree with it and follow it? Can the others in the team be counted on to pull their weight? What's the best way to find out who is good at what? As one candidate said first time round, 'It was difficult: there were 14 natural leaders and no natural followers. Everyone was shouting over everyone else. It was chaos!' With this sort of beginning, it is difficult to get down to business. It is interesting to see what kind of strategies help the winning team succeed – and the pitfalls that challenge the losers.

Danger point: Disorganization

It is important in these tasks that everyone pulls together, and I watch out for that just as I would do in my normal business life. It's vital for company survival that everyone stays alert and understands what is going on. There is a danger that if the team leader does not hold things together the other team members will head off in different directions.

Business lesson: Respecting authority

Disorganization occurs when the team leader is not being clear enough and is allowing more than one star to emerge from the group. Not everyone can be the star of the show. In a competitive situation individuals may feel they have to shine by standing out in order to win the overall prize. That is true to some extent – but if they operate in a way that is at the expense of their colleagues, they fail.

Series 1 – Task 1 result

The first task of Series 1 was to sell flowers on the street. In the girls' team (First Forte) there were seven strong personalities and few team players.

The boys' team agreed a strategy early on and took an 'all-for-one and one-for-all' approach to keep themselves out of the boardroom.

It is interesting in retrospect to notice that the two candidates who stepped up to the plate on Day 1 were eventually to be the first series' finalists.

First Forte team leader: **Saira**
Leading: **Adele, Adenike, Lindsay, Miranda, Miriam, Rachel**

Impact team leader: **Tim**
Leading: **Ben, James, Matthew, Paul, Raj, Sebastian**

Winning strategy

Impact did not spend money on unnecessary trimmings to go with the flowers, and sold hard, door-to-door and in the rain at times. Paul in particular showed his colours as a powerful salesman, and shared his approach with the others.

Winning team:	Impact

| Impact: | £865 = 57% profit |
| First Forte: | £602 = 20% profit |

| In the boardroom: | Saira chose Adenike and Miranda to join her in the boardroom. |

| Fired: | Adenike |

'I am obviously quite a strong-headed person and I like to get my opinion across, especially when things don't seem quite right ... If you're actually fired for supporting the losing strategy – that's fine.'

'I could go out and sell £10 notes for £9 each all day long with no problem I can tell you! But even I wouldn't make a profit.'
SIR ALAN SUGAR – IN THE BOARDROOM

Business lesson 2: Product design –
Innovating versus reinventing an old idea

People in the electronics industry would say, 'Sugar is a gambler. He gambles on products, he gambles on new concepts and he might win six, lose four.' I would agree with them. You have to be a big gambler to win at this game.

But then again, it's not recklessness. It's a case of knowing that the only way to continue to exist is to have something different from giant competitors. And in order to have something different, you've got to gamble to some extent whether something's going to be right or not. I'm certainly not always right. But to offset the risks of gambling on products and development ideas, I've got a huge property portfolio, which is really very safe and boring in comparison.

Calculated risk

Fifteen years ago I woke up to the fact that I had plenty of money, and a family and other commitments – and yet I was a gambler. I thought to myself, 'You've seen how quickly you can make it – and you've also seen how quickly you can lose it.' I mean, one year we lost £70 million. So I decided that I was going to take part of my personal wealth and put it into property. Property is a completely different business. It bores me really. I'm not particularly interested in it at all. It's there to build safe foundations for my family, or for whoever is around me, and for other commitments that I care to make.

Having said that, some people in the property business will say, 'He says it's boring, but he still seems to have some aptitude for the business. He seems to buy the right properties. He doesn't get lumbered with anything – they all seem to be in the right position, they all seem to be let and he doesn't sell anything. He just keeps buying and he doesn't sell anything. So he's not that much of a dummy.'

Well, I'm not saying that because I find it boring I have to be stupid! But I've balanced out the commercial side of my life. I've got businesses like Amstrad and Viglen, the computer operations, where I'm constantly gambling with products and innovation, and on the other side I have become more stable. I've hedged my bets, if you understand me.

It's common knowledge that I am suspicious of people who owe their position to privilege rather than hard work, and I have no respect for those who are simply 'working the system'. That doesn't mean I am against people who come from a different background from my own. That would be ridiculous. What concerns me is when people who don't care about the big picture, who are only interested in immediate personal gain, start to hold positions of influence in business, then the whole marketplace suffers.

How does a company go about designing a new product?

In many instances, especially in the electronics industry, each product evolves from the one that has gone before it. You have to remember that the company concerned is already operating within a defined industry niche, so its profile and products will already be well defined.

Changes in the style and fashion of the product are dictated by the needs of the market. Before spending a vast amount of money on market research, a company is well advised to glean feedback from its sales and marketing teams. What do they want to sell? What pricing level is required? What features are desired?

A study has to be undertaken before spending money on design or development:

- ☛ Can it be made at the preferred price?
- ☛ Is the technology able to do it?
- ☛ Will it be obsolete by the time it comes out?

If the answers are, 'Yes, we can do it in time' and 'Yes, we can meet our pricing criteria', the product is handed over to the designers for tooling a prototype.

All companies need to listen first to what their sales people say before employing market researchers. Salespeople can give you feed-back as to why something is not selling and why something else would sell better. Although in my experience 90 per cent of feedback can be disregarded, 10 per cent is pure gold and something that you can build on.

The next best thing

In our business everything is very much feature-driven. In that way the electronics industry is very like the toy business in that flashing lights and clever gizmos are very appealing to certain customers. In other ways selling computers is more about providing sheer power. There is no point in telling a retailer that no one will ever fill up a 300-gigabyte drive, for example, and that their customers really don't need these. The retailer doesn't care. If the market wants one, the market has to have one. We're constantly chasing our tails to provide the next best thing.

Marketing and technical people need to be aware of how fast technology is moving, and be ready to raise the alert, and even to pull the plug or, if necessary, change the direction of a particular product's development halfway through. But it is very important to decide what the main features are going to be.

The importance of market knowledge

Of course, within the context of the television series, the time con-straints were such that our candidates will be challenged to learn on their feet very quickly in each task, and make maximum use of their expert advisers. When faced with product design for the first time, will they make wise decisions and take the advice of the right people?

The key factors for the team leaders will be to achieve consensus among the team members, to acquire accurate market knowledge and feedback from reputable sources, and to brief their designers effectively and in a focused manner. They need to ensure that the final product will be profitable at less than £10 and will deliver something genuinely new and exciting to the marketplace – quite a challenge.

Innovation versus product enhancements

Very rarely is product design a brand new thing. It's an enhancement of something that has gone before, that the company already has within its existing range of products, or that its competitors have.

If you look at car design, for example, only once every 10 years will the basic body shape change. One manufacturer does it, then all the others follow suit. It is often external factors that dictate a change: for instance, the fuel crisis in the late 1970s saw car design change radically under the Carter administration in the United States. The large gas-guzzlers of the past were gradually surpassed by smaller, more aerodynamic vehicles that offered more speed with less resistance, and therefore greater fuel economy.

The designers' job is to make the product look good once all the basic criteria have been decided upon.

Product design in action

I'm observing the market all the time, and seeing opportunities arising all the time. At Amstrad three or four of us will generally sit down and brainstorm a new idea. We don't have official meetings. We send each other press cuttings, snippets of ideas and information. Each of these triggers a thought that gradually builds into the whole.

I also have a network of contacts in consultancies who are looking at other niches. We exchange ideas about what could be good for this or that. I have people who contact me and say, 'This could be right up your alley … this is just the thing for you.'

I'd like to think that an early Amstrad product could be recognized for its uniqueness in 100 years' time – an electronic antique if you like!

Task 2: Designing a product

CHALLENGE: To create a product from scratch.

AIM: To use brainstorming skills, focus groups and consultancies to judge an unknown market.

RULES AND REGULATIONS

- ☞ The teams have to design a prototype for an original product without using copyrighted images or registered characters.
- ☞ The finished item has to retail at £10 or less.
- ☞ The teams have to make a prototype.
- ☞ The teams each have £300 to buy research materials.
- ☞ They have to pitch their concepts and explain why they will be 'the next big thing'.
- ☞ A product-expert panel will tell me which team, in its opinion, is the winner.

SKILLS TESTED

- ☞ Evaluating a brief.
- ☞ Working with experts.
- ☞ Extracting information from data.
- ☞ Imagination in coming up with new ideas.
- ☞ Pitching an idea.

Evaluating a brief

When evaluating a brief, several critical areas have to be considered: the originality of the idea, the amount of time available, the costs and logistics of developing it, and the price at which it will sell. In most cases a feasibility study will be required, so make sure you approach qualified people for help.

Working with experts

It is important to keep an open mind. As a manufacturer, you can never trust yourself to be the only market expert. You need the cooperation and interest of those who are out there selling the products. In the case of our candidates, who had no knowledge of the market sector at all, it would be important for them to consult those who had industry experience. Note: it is important to remember that you are building professional relationships at all times and to treat people with the respect they deserve.

Extracting information from data

Data should be approached with caution and should not be looked at in isolation from discussion with experts or other market research. It can give an indication of trends, and may reveal whether you are backing an idea that has had its day, but if you are launching a groundbreaking and brand new idea, you won't find an exact match for your product.

Imagination in coming up with new ideas

Received wisdom has it that there is no such thing as a new idea. In many ways that is true. Even the most advanced technological breakthroughs tend to be enhancing a previous product or service. The key, then, is to ensure that your idea has 'legs' in its current manifestation. Test it out on a focus group, make sure that it will be genuinely profitable, and don't over-produce until you have some committed buyers on board.

Pitching a final idea

In order to sell your idea, you need enthusiasm and clarity. Your audience needs to be able to understand clearly what you are offering, both in the context of previous market successes and also in terms of originality, value for money and new features.

In Series 1 our candidates had a few challenges with this task. They weren't short of ideas, but would they choose the right one to put into development? Could it be developed economically? Would they assess the market requirements accurately? The same questions apply no matter which market sector you are entering.

Danger point: Health and safety regulations

We live in increasingly litigious times, and manufacturers are constrained by health and safety considerations. Products need to be made with materials that are non-toxic; components need to be of a size that ensures small children won't swallow or choke on them; polythene bags need to be perforated to avoid suffocation ... and, on top of all that, you need to create something that will have appeal.

Business lesson: Decision-making

It's easy to waste a lot of time on the wrong idea. Listening and a flexible approach are vital to success. It is generally very unwise to insist on a course of action that everyone else is fervently against. It's more usual that 10 people want solution 'A' and three want solution 'B', or the decision is split 50:50.

A leader acts as a sponge really, absorbing information from all quarters. People often think that I don't listen, but I do. I don't miss a trick. I listen to every single thing that is said and I can quote it back when necessary. The art of strong leadership is having the ability to fully appraise a situation and to be decisive. Making the ultimate decision – that's the bottom line. That said, I can't just define a complete strategy for a product and tell people to go away and get on with it.

Series 1 – Task 2 result

This was a favourite task among a few of our candidates, especially those who had never spent time in a design studio before. Perhaps inevitably, given the number of people involved, there was difficulty in reaching consensus on the design. Those with more assertive personalities were definitely starting to take the lead.

The teams (still divided male/female) went to Vivid Toy Manufacturers and Designworks to develop a prototype and packaging for new toys for the children's market. The results were assessed by Vivid, a top toy manufacturer.

First Forte team leader: **Lindsay**
Leading: **Adele, Miranda, Miriam, Rachel, Saira**

Impact team leader: **Raj**
Leading: **Ben, James, Matthew, Paul, Sebastian, Tim**

Winning strategy

The boys' team won easily because the girls' team developed two products instead of one, and their leader then rode roughshod over everyone's opinion to back the weaker idea. Impact had listened to feedback from the toy-making experts and a focus group (a tough audience of boy scouts!) to produce an electronic trading game that was genuinely marketable.

Winning team:	Impact
In the boardroom:	Lindsay chose Adele and Miriam to join her in the boardroom, but there was no contest really. Lindsay had taken what she felt was a courageous decision to back her own idea, but in reality she had disregarded valuable market research and the consistent opinions of her team-mates to back a poor product. In addition, she had wasted professional time by commissioning two prototypes. I had an easy decision to make.
Fired:	Lindsay

'I kind of engineered the boardroom to get Adele sacked because she was the weakest link ... I put Miriam in because she's strong, thinking that that would then give Sir Alan no choice but to fire Adele ... My values are about making a decision and sticking to it. If it's a wrong call, it's a wrong call ...'

'Never rely solely upon market research from your consumers – there is a danger they will tell you what they think you want to hear.'
SIR ALAN SUGAR – IN THE BOARDROOM

Business lesson 3: Discount buying —
How to win at negotiating

When you negotiate, you need to begin with a clear objective in mind. You need to know what you're trying to achieve before you pick up the phone, before you arrange the meeting, before you open your mouth.

Your style of negotiation depends on who you're dealing with – whether you're buying or whether you're selling. Within Amstrad we have a very stable base of suppliers. They don't change a lot because they are mainly component suppliers. So how do we negotiate when our supplier base is relatively static? What we do is set up a proposition. We recognize what motivates the suppliers — what rings their bells.

What normally rings their bells is the anticipation of a big order — and in our case the consistency or the longevity of the order. Doing business with us means that suppliers are not just earning revenue today – they are going to get a consistent amount of business over an extended period of time, and can plan for that revenue stream as part of their annual turnover. Big-volume orders over a long period of time are very attractive to suppliers. We're not just going to turn up tomorrow, buy a few items and never be seen again, so there's a strong proposition around which to build a good negotiation.

Our aim is to negotiate the lowest unit cost possible. Their aim is to get the highest margin on their product.

The usual thing for the purchaser to do when negotiating is to compare what prices the suppliers' competitors are charging for a similar product and to construct an argument that states: while you wish to remain loyal to an existing supplier, you can't ignore what is available in the rest of the world. Of course our candidates don't have the advantage of building long-term relationships — but I watch for how they would begin the business relationship and manage the discussion in the first place.

The importance of supplier relationships

My staff are not the type of people who chop and change suppliers just for the sake of it, or for the short-term gain of a few pennies. If you're thinking of changing suppliers, it's important to give your long-term business partners the opportunity of competing. But first of all you have to weigh up in your own mind whether it's a false economy to jump from one supplier to another. On many occasions, in the long run it will actually cost you more (but perhaps you don't let that be known to the supplier when you're negotiating!).

I've always found that suppliers have got on very well with us over the years. They may not get the right impression initially because we're tough negotiators and we have high expectations. In the long haul, however, if you speak to our suppliers, you'll find that they love us – and the reason is because they get it straight. They don't get any false promises – and if a product is successful, they get repeat orders.

There are, of course, occasions when you might want to wind down some of the supplier commitments you have made. You might be disappointed with their quality, their pricing, their speed of delivery – or you might have found a better supplier elsewhere. In these instances I've always found that honesty is the best policy. Go and see your supplier, tell them your dilemma, tell them the truth of the matter rather than trying to wriggle out with some excuse or by trying to construct an argument that puts the blame on them. They will appreciate your honesty, and may even be able to come up with a solution to the problem or some inside information about their competitor. It is an approach that works – it's always worked for me. Our candidates must speak to business partners with respect in order to achieve an outcome that is mutually beneficial.

A deal is a deal

When we do a deal, it might be a tough deal, and our suppliers might wonder sometimes whether they have a genuinely good deal, but the one thing they can guarantee is that we're going to take the merchandise – and that is not always guaranteed in this business. I don't like people who renege on me, and we certainly don't have a culture of reneging on things that we agree to.

We've made quite a few mistakes in doing deals on certain things, no question about it. Sometimes you have to pay for your mistakes, you have to take the goods and the commitment is paid off. Some of my staff, especially the younger ones, have taken a long time to grasp the logic of this approach. They can't understand sometimes that if things are bad, and you've made a commitment to a supplier, why you continue to take their goods, why you continue to ship them. They've got to understand that you've made a moral commitment. You've made a deal and you just can't ignore that.

As far as I'm concerned, if we've placed an order, I've written a cheque. To my mind, backtracking is the same as bouncing a cheque. What's done is done. I'll go along and talk to the supplier if things are not right, but I won't use tricky means to avoid taking the merchandise.

When things go wrong

Losing out on a deal can feel as if luck has gone against you, but usually, if you look at the situation honestly, you will see where improvements could have been made. Perhaps you were trying to get a good price from a vendor who was not a decision-maker and was therefore unable to negotiate or authorize a discount; perhaps you were trying to buy from the wrong kind of vendor. It is important to get as far back in the supply chain as possible, namely, to the manufacturer, the distributor or the wholesaler, rather than the retailer, in order to negotiate the lowest feasible price.

The reasons for failure will influence future decision-making. Excuses for failure are never acceptable. Excuses are about ducking responsibility and get you nowhere. So make sure when you are taking stock that you find a way of appraising the situation honestly and take steps to improve your methodology in future. This was a message that I had to relay to the Series 1 teams on *The Apprentice* on more than one occasion!

Task 3: Discount buying

CHALLENGE: To buy a list of 10 unrelated, brand items.

AIM: Negotiating the best deal for specified merchandise.

RULES AND REGULATIONS

- The teams use their negotiation skills to purchase 10 items for as low a price as possible.
- They receive £750 for the purchases.
- They return with all the purchased items, receipts and remaining money and an account of their expenses.
- The list price of any items not bought is subtracted from the total.
- The team that spends the least is the winner.

SKILLS TESTED

- Drawing up a purchasing strategy.
- Delegating to the team.
- Talking the vendor down to the cheapest price.

Drawing up a purchasing strategy

Without a strategy, chaos will rule – especially if a number of different purchases need to be made quite fast and in different locations. To purchase effectively requires research: the buyer needs to know what the market prices are and where to get the cheapest stock from, so a good sense of location and timing are critical. Your buyer or buyers need to be in the right place at the right time in order to achieve the optimum deal.

Delegating to the team

The art of delegation is not to give everyone impressive job titles, then leave them to get on with the task. Instead, the team leaders should ensure that they are playing to everyone's strengths. They need to clarify individual roles and make sure they know what their priorities are. It is then essential to stay in regular contact to keep the teams motivated and on track. Only by doing these things can the project be delivered successfully, on time and to budget.

Talking down the price

A vendor will reduce his price only if it brings him a specific benefit. His aim is to make a profit, and he needs to see the advantage of selling at lower than the market price. A good negotiator will be well prepared, will have researched the subject and will be able to set out the advantages of the sale to the vendor.

Danger point: Rebellion and resentment

If you are put in a team reporting to a team leader, it is up to you to get on with delivering the job in hand – and it is up to the team leader to motivate you and other members of the team to deliver. Sometimes you have a person in the team who rebels just for the sake of rebelling. It doesn't matter how much you try to motivate or encourage that person, he or she becomes a semi-saboteur.

Business lesson: Prioritizing

The leader has to stay focused on the task in hand and tackle the problem of rebellion at a later point. There's no point in trying to deal with it on the job because you'll waste valuable time.

After the event you can make your feelings very clear, and unless the person has pretty good reasons for their behaviour, you don't need that kind of individual in your team.

In the tasks set for the Series 1 candidates, I was looking for cooperation. It was the candidates' responsibility to use their best endeavours to follow the leader and deliver to the brief.

Series 1 – Task 3 result

The girls' team had taken a beating in the first two tasks, so I decided to reshuffle the teams to balance the sexes. Adele, as team leader for the girls, selected Tim, Ben and Sebastian to join First Forte. Raj, as team leader for the boys, selected Saira and Rachel to join Impact. The boys were less than happy, but they got on with the job. The girls were delighted at the change, but would it alter the teams' results?

First Forte team leader:	**Adele**
Leading:	**Ben, Miranda, Miriam, Sebastian, Tim**
Impact team leader:	**Matthew**
Leading:	**James, Paul, Rachel, Raj, Saira**

Winning strategy

The new Impact team showed that they were working together effectively. There were some tough negotiators among them, working hard to wear down their suppliers. Saira and Raj notably managed to acquire a freeview box completely free, thus making up for their team-mates failure to buy a new bowler hat. The candidates who were street-smart spoke to mass-market traders rather than up-market retailers – and got better discounts. First Forte became bogged down in bickering and were less successful negotiators, in spite of bringing home all the items.

Winning team: **Impact**

Impact: £447.38 spent on 10 items
First Forte: £506.94 spent on 10 items

In the boardroom: Adele chose Miranda and Ben to join her in the boardroom. It was unclear why Ben was there, but the other two and their bickering ways gave me a headache. The deciding factor was Miranda's attitude of defiance. She had been cast in an inappropriate role as 'personal assistant' to Adele and resented it. As a result, she disregarded the direction of her team leader. That can never be tolerated, so she had to go.

Fired: **Miranda**

'My feelings towards Adele right now aren't really malice ... I'm completely confident with my position and completely thrilled with the experience that I've had.'

'You've given me so many excuses you remind me of my football managers. In fact you've taught them a few tricks!'
SIR ALAN SUGAR – IN THE BOARDROOM

Business lesson 4: Retail management –
Stock selection and sales skills

I haven't been a retailer myself since my earliest days. I wasn't bad at selling, but dealing with the public face to face presents a different kind of challenge from selling business to business. My knowledge of the area comes from my viewpoint as a manufacturer.

In 2004 Amstrad launched the E3 videophone. A lot of work and effort went into the phone, and a lot of learning from past mistakes. We invested in teaching our retailers how to sell the product and took care not to over-produce because the technology changes so fast and suppliers have fixed orders. I knew I'd rather run out than have too many in stock.

A year on, the E3 videophone, as sometimes happens in business, has not been as successful as we hoped – although we will persevere with it. We see it as the starting point of a whole range of technology that we're going to develop. The first version is just a kind of 'seed'. Videophone technology is the way of the future, so we're not despondent, even though the market has not accepted it. We may have been just that little bit too early – as we were on PDAs (Personal Digital Assistants), where we gave up too early, and then someone else took the market. To demonstrate our confidence in the videophone, we're already developing the next version, and are considering the addition of more features to capture the attention of the public. If the next version succeeds and we begin to sell a lot, it will encourage us to think 'What can we do next?'

These days a manufacturer has to battle to get a retailer to take an untested innovative product. The battle normally results in the manufacturer having to let the retailer have stock on some kind of sale or return basis, do some advertising for them, get them in the stores, pay for their point-of-sale material – actually to do all the work for them!

This is quite different from the old retail sales model, where the retailer and manufacturer made decisions in partnership. In the days when great entrepreneurs like Stanley Kalms (founder of Dixons) or Jack Cohen (founder of Tesco) were around, a manufacturer like me, who was good at manufacturing, would speak to a retailer like them, who was good at retailing, and there was no need to have to convince anyone else – they saw it for themselves. They would want the new product straight away – sometimes the whole lot!

If I want an opinion these days I am unlikely to go to one of the high-street chains: instead I will go to a privately owned store, large or small, because I want to speak to a business person who owns the shop, who is operating at the front line, whose personal profit margin depends upon the stock-buying decisions that are made. Someone who touches the merchandise, feels it, is on the doorstep all the time – they know! You show him or her something and they can give you an honest answer straight away.

The key business lesson in retail management relates to the choice and range of product. This needs to be combined with careful attention to floor display and signage. As ever, location is everything. The candidates will experience their retail task in one of the most successful stores in London. They have access to highly talented and well-trained retail managers, and will have every opportunity to make the day a success.

Task 4: Running a retail department

CHALLENGE: To run a given area of a department store.

AIM: To choose a range of appropriate products at a price range that allows maximum profit.

This is a high-calibre task for the candidates, and a true test of business acumen and grit under pressure. Focus and effective product selection are the keys to success. Which team will win, and how?

RULES AND REGULATIONS

☛ The teams select products to sell from a list of goods provided by the store. They cannot sell anything that is not on the list.

☛ Each team has a seed fund of £600 to spend as it sees fit. All spending on the task days has to be drawn from this fund.

☛ The teams have to abide by the store's trading rules at all times.

☛ The store keeps track of what has been sold. The team with the highest turnover is the winner.

SKILLS TESTED

☛ Product selection.

☛ Delegation.

☛ Flexibility.

☛ Calmness under pressure.

Product selection

When I briefed the Series 1 candidates I reminded them that they needed to look at making high-volume sales. This did not necessarily mean stocking up with low-priced goods. The major lesson for all involved was that less is often more: in this particular case, fewer product lines could well mean more money.

Delegation

This was a task that required effective team playing. There was a lot to juggle and the days were long. There was no space for slacking, raised voices or disrespectful behaviour. A team leader in this situation needs to remain calmly confident, upbeat and organized. There was definitely no room for complacency.

Flexibility

While strategy and planning are very important, having contingency plans is also essential. This means that if things don't go according to plan, survival techniques are still possible. Retail selling is full of surprises.

James's team (Impact) changed their tactics when they saw how well their opponents were apparently doing. Entertainment was suddenly added to their armoury: Paul dressed up as 'Rosie Bear' and came to the rescue. With his enthusiastic involvement, the sales improved dramatically.

Calmness under pressure

Leaders need to keep calm in order to inspire. The teams needed to keep calm for the good of each other. People's ability to remain calm can often be measured by how they speak to third parties. Let's just say that some candidates are more diplomatic than others.

Danger point: Appropriate price range

This is a task which operates within a tight timeframe. It is important that the teams chose the right goods at the right prices to attract the sector of the public likely to be drawn to the department. In Series 1, Impact felt that their inexperience showed that their range of product choices had room for improvement, so they redoubled their efforts and both teams used gift vouchers as a discount incentive to shift as much stock as possible.

Business lesson: Distinguishing luck from hard work

A lot of people say that business success is founded on luck, and of course there is an element of luck involved in certain deals and on certain days. If you are in the right place at the right time and something occurs that is completely unexpected and unplanned that you benefit from, then of course luck plays its part. But there is no such thing as luck in long-term business. There is just hard work, determination and knowing what your business is all about.

Luck was debated quite hard in one of the tasks as playing its part for one of the teams. It might be tempting to agree, but usually there are other factors at play that contribute to success, such as effective planning and choice of products, pricing, display and selling skills. Because contestants had some success, a lot of people termed it 'luck'.

Series 1 – Task 4 result

Mohammed El Fayed is a personal friend of mine. He and his staff were doing us a great favour by allowing us to host one of our tasks in his Harrods store: 1 million square feet; seven floors; 330 departments; 56 buyers. I made it clear from the outset that his staff were to be treated with respect.

The day had its fair share of drama. One of the team leaders acknowledged that 'The task was a complete shambles first thing this morning.' Such high feeling, and all they had been asked to do was set up shop at the most prestigious retail outlet in the UK, if not the world!

First Forte team leader: **Tim**
Leading: **Adele, Ben, Miriam, Sebastian**

Impact team leader: **James**
Leading: **Matthew, Paul, Rachel, Raj, Saira**

Winning strategy

The results could not have been much closer, but the truth is that the winning team showed themselves to be tenacious and calm under pressure, with the ability to sell with determination, flair and focus. Saira didn't stop selling, flat out, until the whistle blew – and her final sale clinched the win.

Winning team:	Impact	

Turnover

	Halfway through task	At close of task
Impact:	£2,141	£3,295.38
First Forte:	£1,659	£3,108.50

In the boardroom: Tim's choice of who to take with him to the boardroom was taken out of his hands when Adele chose to resign. She had picked up on my criticism of her attitude and saw the writing on the wall. I made it clear that she would have gone that week anyway. Her attitude had been disrespectful to others in her team and to the staff at Harrods. It was a shame. She was a bright girl and I had high hopes of her.

Fired: Adele

'I was the easy target ... I am a lot of competition because I've got a very entrepreneurial background, and that was a threat.'

'A business lesson for all to learn is that fewer product lines can mean more money.'
SIR ALAN SUGAR – IN THE BOARDROOM

Business lesson 5: Closing the deal –
Focusing on the bottom line

A specialist in a particular field may tell you that it is important to educate customers in order to persuade them to buy. I think that is nonsense. There are broadly three types of customer:

- Those who will make an impulse purchase.
- Those who don't understand what to buy and need some guidance.
- Those who don't necessarily like what they are buying, but are already well informed.

In my view you can't talk someone into buying anything. What you need to do is sense whether you have someone sniffing at the bait. That is where the talent comes in. Watch your customer's body language, spot whether someone has a genuine interest, and set about closing the deal.

Being condescending and schmoozy won't wash anywhere, whether in the refined environment of the arts or out there on the high street. Trying to persuade someone what they ought to be buying is the wrong way to go about it.

Connoisseurs of every industry tend to be rather po-faced and want to be left alone to make their own decisions. If you can detect this kind of person, it is best just to wait and listen, and to be ready to answer questions. Hopefully, their first question will be 'How much?' If their response in non-committal or negative, it is time to find out what the obstacle is. It may be that the price needs to go down a bit in order to clinch the deal.

There are others who will buy because they want to buy, but just don't know whether something is good or not. You can exploit that by giving them some facts to help them make an informed decision.

How do you tell who the real buyers are? At a launch event it can be tricky for the inexperienced to tell the difference between a buyer and a 'hanger-on' because there are many people who will be attracted by the ambience and the champagne and canapés. The candidates were faced with this scenario and would have found the distinction hard. But a few good opening questions should indicate fairly quickly whether the guests are potential buyers or not: 'Are you here to buy this evening? What kind of product do you usually buy?'

My own belief is that selling is an instinct that relates to some form of knowledge that is innate in you. It's a kind of in-built sensitive intelligence that helps you sense and understand; something you were born with and you can build on and learn to use through experience. I instinctively know, and I have always known, when I have someone on the hook. I know when I've got a deal, and when you find yourself in this situation you have to close the deal there and then. If there is an obstacle, you need to detect it straight away. What is the deal-breaker?

The last thing you should do is let the customer go away and think about it or talk about it. You want to get a commitment, so you just keep hammering away at the obstacles, either subtly or not so subtly, depending upon your customer. If a business transaction does go on for days, so you have to learn to hold your nerve, not make that final call, otherwise you come across as too anxious.

What is instinct?

I believe that instinct is innate, something you are born with, but also something that you can build on, that you can learn through experience. It's a kind of inbuilt sensitive intelligence that helps you to see and understand things without being conscious of it. There are some amongst the candidates who have this skill and others who find it hard. It is satisfying to watch some candidates discover a skill they don't know they have, and to watch others hone their ability in different business scenarios.

The silent close

In selling there is a tough device used, which is called 'the silent close'. Any salesperson these days who has been on a training course will know about it. In the silent close you stay silent in order to force the other person to talk. A deliberate silence may last only a few seconds, but it might feel as if it has gone on for hours.

A silent close is usually used after the point when you have proffered your best deal, and you're implying, 'I don't mean to be rude, but I'm going now – this is your last chance.' You only come to understand how to use silence in negotiating by using it.

In my industry there is no point in selling something to someone if they don't want it or need it. It is a principle that will hold broadly true for every other sector as well.

Task 5: The art challenge

CHALLENGE: To select a marketable artist and host a private view.
AIM: Achieve a match between saleability and profitability.

RULES AND REGULATIONS

- ☛ Both teams visited the same list of artists, then decided who they wanted to represent.
- ☛ As both teams chose the same artist, the artist decided who would represent him or her.
- ☛ The teams worked with the artists to decide on prices for display and sale.
- ☛ The teams had to sell as much artwork as possible.

SKILLS TESTED

- ☛ Understanding popular choice.
- ☛ Making a profitable decision.
- ☛ Trusting judgement.
- ☛ Credibility in a closed commercial world.
- ☛ Getting potential customers through the door.
- ☛ Optimizing the team's effectiveness.

Understanding popular choice
Art selection can be quite daunting, and the art world can be intimidating to those unused to it. Taste in art is very personal, and opinions about artistic works are deeply subjective – yet, as with all sales tasks, normal rules apply. It's whether your buyers like the product that matters. Of course, it's easier to sell if you like it too.

Making a profitable decision

Do you select low-priced art and opt for high turnover, or do you aim for the high end of the marketplace and recognize that you have to sell for the long haul? Our Series 1 teams considered both options. This assignment was a tough one because only two of the artists were priced at a level to make big money. Both teams liked one of these; the other artist's work was disliked by Paul and Matthew because they felt it was pornographic. Rachel as team leader disagreed, but felt they needed to go with someone that everyone felt comfortable selling.

Trusting judgement

Body language always plays a part in selling, but in the art arena it is especially important. James from Series 1 was very comfortable in this world and better able to judge the selling potential than some of the more seasoned salespeople among the candidates. How would the artists weigh up our teams and decide who they wanted to represent them? How would our salespeople decide who to approach, and what was the right length of time to wait to close a deal?

Credibility in a closed commercial world

Surprisingly, Saira and Paul, who had shone the most brightly as salespeople in earlier tasks, found that their skills were not as effective in this new arena. Paul in particular found marked differences between this style of selling and what he was used to: 'I couldn't go in for the kill very early, or close early.'

Getting potential customers through the door

How would you go about getting the art-buying public over your threshold? Suave determination and the promise of an exciting evening? Or would the hard sell be more effective? Once through the door, how do you ensure everyone is attended to and that no potential buyers slip away? It is definitely a team effort, and there needs to be clear communication and flexibility all round.

Optimizing the team's effectiveness
Deciding who will connect best with the purchasers and how best to keep the teams motivated if sales are slow – these are the challenges to be tackled. This task offers one of the most interesting examples of how to combine different styles of sales techniques and keep cool under pressure, and it assesses whether the candidates will stay focused on profit or get caught up with assessing artistic talent. It was good to see so many of the Series 1 candidates putting into practice the lessons learnt previously.

Danger point: Working as a team

In some businesses, such as the jewellery trade, the clothing industry and the art market, it can sometimes be useful to have more than one seller working in partnership. One person operates as the so-called 'expert'. This may be the diamond technician, or the fashion consultant, or, in the case of art, the art 'historian'. It is important that the technical salesperson is divorced from closing the deal. They do not need to talk about money – they are there to advise.

Salesperson number two can then take on the role of the closer. 'Did you find my colleague helpful?' They can explore the price categories and what might suit their customer's budget.

If both sides of the sales partnership are working together consciously, each will acknowledge what the other has contributed and will say that they were equally responsible for the deal. In a less cooperative situation that acknowledgement will not be forthcoming.

Business lesson: Keeping an eye on the bottom line

When you're selling a product that is unique and variable, such as art or crafts, it can be hard to remember that the aim is still to make a profit and that the profit margin is still the key to business success.

Series 1 – Task 5 result

The teams were uneven in number again, so I asked Sebastian, as team leader of First Forte, to choose a member of Impact to join his side. The candidates had got to know each other quite well by this time, so I was interested in the choice made. It was to be James: calm-headed diplomat and smooth negotiator. A wise choice as it turned out because he helped First Forte towards their first win.

First Forte team leader:	**Sebastian**
Leading:	**Ben, James, Miriam, Tim**
Impact team leader:	**Rachel**
Leading:	**Matthew, Paul, Raj, Saira**

Winning strategy

The winning team launched a charm offensive on their preferred artists and encouraged them to fully demonstrate their work. They were able to convince them of their ability to sell and represent their work more effectively than the other team, and they went on to mingle and sell very assertively. In truth, once they had secured the most profitable artist, they were halfway to success. They had to sell only one painting to beat the other team. That was a challenge in itself.

Winning team:	**Impact**
First Forte:	£19,563.75
Impact:	£6,147.50
In the boardroom:	Rachel opted to take Matthew and Paul with her to the boardroom. There were faults on all sides, but Matthew's attitude was beginning to show up as his Achilles' heel. A nice guy, but hard work as a team member, it was time for him to go.
Fired:	**Matthew**
	'I knew it was going to happen ... it was inevitable. If he doesn't want an original thinker in his company ... that's his problem.'

'At the end of the day ... it is the people that tend to be a bit more pushy that get noticed more.'
SIR ALAN SUGAR – IN THE BOARDROOM

Business lesson 6: Advertising –
Marketing and branding

Advertising for Amstrad needs a certain style. We are straightforward in approach, with no need for fancy punchlines or catchy jingles, so on balance we tend to create our own adverts in house. Our advertising style reflects my own style: it tends to be straightforward and 'in your face'.

Advertising companies make little money from media-selling these days – that's all done via the media buyers. They win by charging for their creative skills. We prefer to work with our own ideas. As the technology has become easier to use, we decided that we could do our own advertisements – with the right technical partners – so we sit with the technicians and create what we want.

What does marketing mean exactly? It is the opposite of direct selling and is more to do with brand awareness – making the public aware of the product. If you are a manufacturer, dependent upon a retailer to sell your product, marketing is about making it easier for that retailer to sell your product.

There are many companies that focus on building a brand. Amstrad has never adopted that approach. How would we market the brand? 'Always Innovating', offering products that are 'Best Value for Money' and 'Packed Full of Features' – but our products change. Our marketing is therefore much more about building awareness of our products.

There are no big marketing budgets in electronics because the products have a relatively short lifespan and therefore a slim profit margin, compared with something like baked beans, for example. If a product such as baked beans makes a tremendous profit margin, there will be financial resources available to run a periodic and probably costly advertising campaign just to remind the public that the brand is still out there, even though, generally speaking, the sales curve remains safe and steady.

Sports products have a different pricing model and are interesting for a different reason. Here the unit cost of production is very low but the vast percentage of the budget goes on marketing – the reason being that in order to sell the product, the manufacturers need to build brand awareness. The only way to do this is via continuous and costly advertising.

Electronic products rarely command the kind of margin that justifies a large marketing budget. If the product has only a certain sales volume, therein lies the profit margin and the budget for promoting it. At Amstrad we design our advertising in house and we keep it simple, focusing on features and value-for-money pricing.

I was interested to see what the Series 1 teams would put together for this task and to see whether they would remember basic commercial principles or get carried away in a storm of creativity.

Task 6: Creating an advertising campaign

CHALLENGE: To produce an advertising campaign.

AIM: To establish an instant market for a never-before-seen product. To think of how to pitch a campaign, design and present it.

RULES AND REGULATIONS

☞ The teams are briefed and asked to design an ad campaign for a new product.

☞ Each team has a budget of £1000.

☞ They brief themselves on the product by trying to use it, and work out the possible markets it is aimed at.

☞ As a minimum, they have to produce one print advert and a 30-second television advert.

☞ The teams present the campaign proposal: the strongest campaign is the winner.

SKILLS TESTED

☞ Evaluating a complex brief.

☞ Imagination in coming up with new ideas.

☞ Understanding of the market.

☞ Pitching an idea.

☞ Communicating an idea to professional creatives.

Evaluating a complex brief
When faced with a brief it is important to decide what the priorities are, and in business that's easy. It's finance – starting with the budget. In turn, the budget is driven by the bottom line. If we are selling a specific item that has a fashionable shelf-life of, say, 18 months, we've got to sell a certain quantity over that period. The quantity that we sell has to equate to a gross margin,

and that gross margin will let you know how much you've got left for your advertising budget. Simple really, but not all our Series 1 candidates saw it that way.

Imagination in coming up with new ideas
A lot of people think of themselves as creative, and brainstorming is a favourite occupation in most organizations. The challenge comes when you are surrounded by 100 different ideas and have to decide which of them has 'legs'. If you are running a theme through a variety of different media, it is important to ensure that the central concept has a simplicity and clarity for the punters to understand. We have a number of creative thinkers among our teams, but the challenge is to keep the ideas grounded in order to convey the central message.

Understanding of the market
An advert needs to convey the right message to the market sector that is actually going to purchase the product. Children's advertising is probably the most blatant, telling you what the features of the products are, how much fun it's going to be to play with and how much it costs.

Advertising is so often a self-indulgence. I get irritated by watching adverts that are meaningless, and so far removed from the product they are selling that they fail to convey any information. Advertising has become an art form in its own right – and an entertainment. Presumably, companies with big budgets get a return on their investment, but in some instances, frankly, I'd be surprised. In my world we keep it simple: we identify who'll buy the product and we speak to them directly and in a way that informs.

There were some bright people on our Series 1 teams with some solid sales experience, so I was pretty confident that they would keep their objective in mind. The results were very interesting.

Pitching an idea
Advertising has a very short period in which to make an impact. It is usually the repetition of exposure that hooks the buyer. If the person with the concept can sell it and get others to buy into it, then it is likely to fly. With so many creative players around the table, I am interested to find out who listens to whom and how they reach team consensus regarding a marketable concept.

Communicating an idea to professional creatives
Professional creatives are a crucial part of your team. They are among the first people who truly need to buy into your concept. If they don't get it, either change your designer (early on) or, if you respect the professional's opinion, think again.

It is important to remember that designers, typographers and photographers are talented people who have skills that you don't have. They also have a visual sense that will bring something extra to the table – but it is still not their project. Designers need space to be creative, but need your guidance to ensure that the look works for the marketplace. My advice would always be not to move too far away from your designer, and to keep yourself involved in the process. Mistakes can be expensive, and that cost is coming off your bottom-line profit.

Danger point: Negotiating with a jobs-worth

It's very rare these days to have main dealings with someone who is at a sufficiently senior level to have the complete view, so it is usually middle management that you come up against. It is rare at that level to find someone who will take risks.

In order to deal effectively with jobs-worths and blockers, it's important to pre-empt and overcome the obstacles in their minds. Build them a big fat comfort-pillow on which to make a decision; then you'll have them onside. Don't ask them to take risks, because your competitors may come along later and be more ready to bend to their rules, which will leave them with the commercial advantage.

Business lesson: Managing difficult people

Personality clashes are a fact of life. I don't expect to like everyone I work with, and I don't expect everyone who works for me to like each other, but I do expect them to work together in an effective and professional manner.

If communication breaks down, the business suffers. If the differences are irreconcilable, I take a good look at the individuals' personal qualities and do what I can to keep them apart. Of course, if one of those people is rubbing a lot of staff up the wrong way, I have a problem, and that person has to go.

Series 1 – Task 6 result

This task was a real test of strategic ability and team management. And the item to be promoted was one of mine, which added to the teams' pressure!

First Forte team leader:	**Miriam**
Leading:	**Ben, James, Sebastian, Tim**
Impact team leader:	**Paul**
Leading:	**Rachel, Raj, Saira**

Winning strategy

The winning strategy was clear and simple. First Forte decided on a coherent theme, chose a strapline for the theme, and integrated the two in a clear and focused way. As a result, both the video and the print ad featured the same themes. By contrast, Impact did not act in a coherent fashion: communication broke down, the team leader didn't communicate her intentions, and the result was an unprofessional muddle.

Winning team:	**First Forte**
In the boardroom:	Paul took Saira and Rachel with him to the boardroom. I gave them all a hard time. Paul hadn't managed his team; Saira had left her designer alone to produce an appalling print ad, but it was Rachel who disappointed me the most. Her contribution was completely out of place in a commercial setting, and on top of that she had misjudged the mood of the commercial panel.
Fired:	Rachel
	'Perhaps I just didn't stand up for myself loudly enough.'

'I've written books on advertising. You might not find them for sale on the Internet, cos they're cheque books – big fat cheque books!'
SIR ALAN SUGAR – IN THE BOARDROOM

Business lesson 7: Innovation and managing people — *Influencing, fund-raising and entertainment*

This task took on different guises in the two series. In Series 1 the lesson had a celebrity fund-raising focus. In Series 2 (Task 10) it has a commercial money-making focus, but is still concerned with entertainment.

Like many people in the public eye, I am approached daily with requests for money, appearances and various other favours. Many of them are immediately filed in the dustbin. Spreading money thinly just doesn't work. Giving a large donation to a single charity is more effective than giving small amounts to several. But I am careful to make sure that 80 per cent of the donation isn't spent on supporting the infrastructure of the charity.

There are many thousands of wannabe Apprentices who would have walked 100 miles to take part in the next task facing the teams, just for the opportunity of meeting celebrities. But what appears to be a glamorous job on the surface usually represents a great deal of extremely hard work behind the scenes – as our Series 1 teams found out.

The real task here was to handle people effectively. Celebrities are people who are in the public eye a great deal and whose larger-than-life personalities can need careful handling. They are people who can spot a time-waster at 100 yards, who are approached on a regular basis by people who want things from them. Celebrities are often under a great deal of pressure themselves.

Having gained the attention of their celebrities, our intrepid candidates then had to convince them to participate in the task.

How should you handle a celebrity?

When speaking to someone who is bombarded daily with requests, to have their attention at all means that you are 70 per cent there. The candidates had to watch the body language, however, to make sure they had the celebrities' attention and were not irritating them.

In general the guidelines are:

- ☛ Crank up the sales pitch if you are talking to a 'soft' person.
- ☛ Go into 'listening' mode if speaking to a tougher customer.
- ☛ Be yourself.

I am often confronted with people who feel they need to imitate what they perceive to be my gruffness of approach when they want something from me. They will adopt an aggressive and belligerent manner, which, frankly, will get them nowhere fast. Play-acting annoys me at the best of times, but this 'wide-boy' approach irritates me most of all. Anyone with an aggressive attitude is kicked out immediately. People who gain my attention tend to get to the point as quickly as possible, are logical, honest and straightforward. The same principles will apply to most people.

Task 7: Charity auction of celebrity promises

CHALLENGE: To persuade celebrities to make contributions towards a fund-raising event (raising funds for Hackney Empire).

AIM: To negotiate, organize and deliver.

RULES AND REGULATIONS

☛ The two team leaders were presented with a list of celebrities.

☛ The teams researched their celebrities and discovered what they might offer. They had to schedule meetings and meet their celebrities face to face to negotiate for their time.

☛ They chaperoned their celebrities to the venue, and the winning team was the one that raised the most money.

SKILLS TESTED

☛ Negotiation.

☛ Diplomacy.

☛ Charm under pressure.

☛ Ability to add value.

☛ Organization.

☛ Delegation.

Negotiation

Negotiating with someone in the public eye is no different from negotiating with anyone anywhere else. However, acute attention to the person's body language is needed, and, owing to time constraints, it is important to be well prepared and aim to close the discussion with an agreed action as quickly as possible.

Diplomacy

Tactfulness is always important, and those in the public eye are likely to reject inappropriate, downright rude or ill-informed approaches. Be polite. Be sensitive. Be clear. Be honest. You will get a far better response.

Charm under pressure

Celebrities have, in the main, turned charm under pressure into a professional skill. You may feel as if you are under pressure, but it is nothing compared to their experience of being constantly in the public eye, so keep calm and keep smiling.

Ability to add value

The art of selling includes being able to add value to the simplest item. If the item has belonged to a celebrity, that is your added value. It is important to understand the value of what you are selling and what your market will pay for it. If you have a wealthy audience who have come to spend money, the value of the goods you are selling needs to match the expectations and lifestyle of your audience.

Organization

Plan your task. Plan how you would like it to go. If you are the team leader, communicate the plan to your team and ensure you have their support and backing. Once these preparations are in place, make at least one contingency plan because when you're dealing with other people – especially celebrities – nothing ever goes entirely as you expect it to.

Delegation

Bear in mind that whatever the task, it is always important for each member of the team to know what is expected of them and to act accordingly. Acting as a team does not mean doing everything together; that just leads to confusion.

Danger point: Thinking small

When speaking to famous people, there can be a tendency for awe of their fame to get in the way and make you miss the opportunity of gaining the 'big prize'. It's important to know who you are speaking to, to listen carefully to what they are saying and to recognize both their 'market value' and what the general public most values about them. If you have got as far as winning the interest of someone whose fame can help raise funds, there is little point in using the opportunity to gain something you could have achieved without their input.

Business lesson: Effective briefing

When selling through a third party, whether a salesperson, a retailer or an auctioneer, it is crucially important to remember that yours is unlikely to be the only product they are selling. A salesperson rarely has longer than three minutes to make a pitch, and frequently has to make a positive sales impact with a single sentence. It is up to the individual briefing the salesperson to ensure that they understand the unique selling point of the item and that they have been given a helpful one-liner with which to sell it.

Series 1 – Task 7 result

The restoration of Hackney Empire is a cause close to my heart, so it felt good to host a task that would raise funds for it, irrespective of which team won. As happens from time to time in companies, it was becoming clear that two of the candidates, Paul and Saira, were suffering from a personality clash that was in danger of sabotaging their success and that of others. I decided to separate them, and the reshuffle changed the dynamic of both teams. The new teams became:

| First Forte team leader: | James |
| Leading: | Raj, Saira, Sebastian |

| Impact team leader: | Ben |
| Leading: | Miriam, Paul, Tim |

Winning strategy

The winning team seemed to know their celebrities rather better than the losers, but the bottom line on this occasion was that they were the more effective negotiators and closed deals more convincingly. Team leader Ben was not afraid to 'think big' and raised the game of those with him. They also used humour effectively and respectfully towards those they dealt with. On the night of the auction they took time to mingle with the crowd, pitching their lots and firing up enthusiasm for the event. They realized that at an auction a sale is not complete until the hammer has fallen.

Their master lot was a Suzuki 600 motor bike contributed by Diarmuid Gavin that sold for £6000.

Winning team:	Impact
Impact:	£10,000 raised
First Forte:	£18,000 raised

In the boardroom: James took Raj and Sebastian with him to the boardroom. It was pretty clear that the team could have been more bullish in their expectations of what they could reasonably have asked of the celebrities. By this point in the series I was expecting everyone to have found their voice. I wasn't getting any sense of Sebastian's contribution, and was finding his reticence hard to take. He was a charming man, but would not fit my companies' culture. He had under-performed on this task, and it was time for him to go.

Fired: Sebastian

'I wasn't expecting to go quite now.'

'I need closers! I need do-ers!'
SIR ALAN SUGAR – IN THE BOARDROOM

Business lesson 8: Margins — *Controlling your costs*

One of the most important aspects of any business is to keep an eye on costs. Monthly, even weekly, I check that we are covering our costs and that we are selling our goods at the right price. This is the single most important thing in our business.

We make sure that we are keeping the costs of our materials down to the level we have planned for, and that our overheads and manufacturing costs are not running away with themselves. If they are increasing in cost, we have to increase our prices (which does not happen very often, I might add).

This task tests the ability of the candidates to keep their eye on the bottom line.

Key questions to ask
- What is the product?
- Which product will sell the best?
- What kind of pricing do you want to sell the product for?
- What kind of margin are you looking for?
- How much are you going to spend on organization?

The amount you have to spend on manufacturing the product is determined by what's left over from your organization costs.

I know it sounds too easy when put like that, but it really is that simple; and yet you would be amazed at how many people start at the wrong end of the process, or just don't see it at all.

At Amstrad the first thing we establish when we set out to make a product is how much we can sell it for. If the team considers that the top-end price is £99, there you have it — the first stake in the ground. From that point you work backwards to calculate your ideal margin, VAT, dealer margin, the cost of designing and building a prototype, production and overheads. Once you've stripped all that out, what's left is the amount you have to spend on materials. Simple.

If you go about it the wrong way round and focus on design first and costs afterwards, you are a slave to price – and whether you price high or low, you will still lose a load of money. I'd be watching out for that on this task.

The bottom line is: if you cannot afford to buy the components, you can't afford to make the product. In an ideal world I would create a car that runs on water and sell it for £1000 a time, but it's just not possible. In the electronics business you can't afford to make a product that is featureless. In a farmers' market (the Series 1 scenario) you won't get repeat business if you produce a product that is flavourless. You need to be aware that with any idea you might get to a point where you just have to walk away.

Task 8: Maximizing profits at a farmers' market

CHALLENGE: To add value to basic ingredients by creating food products to sell at a farmer's market.

AIM: To make the maximum margin.

RULES AND REGULATIONS

- The teams had to research, develop and manufacture food product(s) for sale.
- Each team had seed money of £750.
- They had to source and buy their raw ingredients.
- They had to process, brand and package the produce to increase its value.
- They had to supply full accounts and paperwork for this task on the sheets provided.

SKILLS TESTED

- Sourcing.
- Exercising cost control.
- Researching competitors.
- Pricing.
- Maximizing profit margins.

There was experience of catering across the Series 1 teams of candidates, so this task was an interesting mix of general ability combined with expertise.

The challenge on this occasion was not to maximize takings, but to make the largest profit margin – that critical space between cost of sales and turnover. There was also the challenge of dealing with lots of goods that would quickly exceed their sell-by date.

The big temptation when entering the food industry is to treat catering the way you would a dinner party. You want the best for your guests and you want everyone to compliment you and come back for more. This is all well and good, but in the commercial world you need to make sure that the reason people are coming back for more is down to good value and good quality, rather than superior quality for the price and too much value for money.

Effective stock control is crucial. Simplicity is essential. Too many product lines can be a mistake, and it is also important not to spend too much on your basic ingredients.

Danger point: Deciding on your budget

Buying ingredients or materials without first deciding what your profit margin should be is rather like going on a shopping spree without checking your bank balance first. It is a high-risk strategy. Budget is crucial.

Business lesson: Margin is king

As elsewhere in business, profit margin is king in catering. The place to check for potential profit is not in the day's takings, but in the amount of food that is wasted. Did our candidates grasp this crucial point?

Series 1 – Task 8 result

After seven weeks of intensive work in London I'm sure the teams were quite pleased to be dispatched to the countryside for some fresh air! Their task was to focus on profit margin by producing foodstuffs for sale at a London-based farmers' market. Raj's team were up at dawn picking cost-free ingredients from the hedgerows. Ben's team spent their seed money on luxury ingredients, such as venison and Stilton.

First Forte team leader: **Raj**
Leading: **James, Saira**

Impact team leader: **Ben**
Leading: **Miriam, Paul, Tim**

Winning strategy

First Forte started off by over-committing their budget, but recognized their error early on and focused on recipes that used natural (free) ingredients from the hedgerows, and persuaded a talented cook to work with them for free in exchange for leaflet advertising. Hard selling combined with tasty, well-priced product and good humour helped them to sell all their stock at the market – at a profit.

Winning team:	First Forte
First Forte:	£384.35 profit (£78 spent on ingredients)
Impact:	£149.69 profit (£274 spent on ingredients)

In the boardroom: Ben took Paul and Miriam with him to the boardroom. There was a lot of evasiveness amongst the three, and it was hard to get to the bottom of who had been responsible for the overspending on ingredients. A lot of fingers were pointed at Miriam, but at the root of the matter was the lack of a designated budget and Ben's apparent lack of awareness of the need for one. In my business I need budget-awareness, so Ben went home.

Fired: Ben

'What have I learned? I've learned that I don't like retail, and I don't like pumpkin soup!'

'Always start off with a target margin. Without knowing that you are dead in the water.'
SIR ALAN SUGAR – IN THE BOARDROOM

Business lesson 9: Direct selling –
The challenge of selling face to face

This is the greatest challenge to date for our six remaining candidates. If you were faced with a captive audience of 36,000 people (as our Series 1 teams were), how would you grab their attention? This assignment is described as marketing, but is, in fact, a challenging face-to-face sales task. The solutions our candidates come up with need to be inventive, creative and carefully planned.

The problem with advertising – in print or on TV – is that it costs a great deal because you have to place ads consistently. This ensures that the message enters consumer consciousness gradually, irrevocably, over a long period of time. On average, it takes three or four airings for a consumer to notice an advert. Leaflets are all very well. They are useful for making paper aeroplanes, for example! Punters will often take a leaflet from a vendor because it's easier than saying no and walking away.

I told the Series 1 candidates that their assignment was a businessman's dream. The commodity that they had to sell was tailored exactly to the 36,000 fans gathered in the Tottenham Hotspur football stadium: a telephone text messaging service that would text news about the club to subscribers' phones. The team to sell the most subscriptions would win

The key point here was that the fans were in a positive mood. They wanted things to go well. They were feeling optimistic. They were in just the frame of mind to be sold to. Our candidates had something to sell and they had the customers in the palm of their hands.

How do you sell to them? You connect with them. Talk, talk, talk – you don't stop talking. In Series 1 Saira did rather a lot of that – using a megaphone.

Careful planning, knowing your product and the competition, and targeting the customer with the right information are crucial when selling direct. If you are looking for high value, you need to target the right sector of people, and make sure you make their decision easy. If your own business is dependent upon sales and you have direct contact with your customers, my advice would be stay with them face to face until the deal is made. Marketing material has great value, but is at its most effective when you are there to pitch it to them – so keep talking!

Implicit in this direct face-to-face selling task was the need to keep an eye on how things were going. When you have only nine hours to achieve results, you need to remain very flexible. You need to assess what is working, and to change tack fast if you think you are not getting results. But to do that you need to keep an eye on your sales progress during the selling period, and alter your tactics quickly if you are not getting the sales.

Task 9: Marketing a product

CHALLENGE: To sell a mobile phone text messaging service to Tottenham Hotspur supporters.

AIM: To sell services with no visible product while under time pressure.

RULES AND REGULATIONS

☞ The teams had to sign up new customers.

☞ Each team had to design a competition and/or promotion to attract subscribers, erect a stand in the building concourse and obtain uniforms.

☞ Each team had £2,000 seed money.

☞ The teams were responsible for ensuring that their plans abided by health and safety regulations.

☞ The winning team was the one that obtained the most subscriptions.

SKILLS TESTED

☞ Entrepreneurial flair.

☞ Ability to persuade customers to sign.

☞ Remaining calm in high-pressure conditions.

☞ Optimizing a location.

☞ Teamwork.

Entrepreneurial flair

Each of the candidates had entrepreneurial flair, but which of them would cope best with face-to-face pressure on the day, combined with cold weather and a host of other challenges? You need to be inventive and persistent when faced with a large crowd of people. You need to grab attention and add the entertainment factor. This task brought out the best and the worst in our candidates. There were some very inventive and effective marketing ideas on the table. The candidates I expected to shine did not necessarily rise to the occasion; others became hungry for a win and cut right to the chase in order to achieve their objective.

Ability to persuade customers to sign

Slick talk and long-term marketing plans are all very well, but we were looking for sign-ups on the day. How would the candidates plan their attack? How would they prioritize the markets to focus on? How well would they operate as a team? And, face to face with the customer, would the candidates be able to clinch the sale on the spot or let the deal slip away?

Remaining calm in high-pressure conditions

Panic spreads, so in any business situation self-discipline is the order of the day. Feeling out of your depth? Use the feeling as motivation to get better informed. Having an off-day? Focus on lifting your team-mates so that their positive enthusiasm pulls you through. Saira as team leader was not at her best and confessed to some personal issues. The question was, did this affect the overall team performance? It's always a difficult call. Frustrated that the best-laid plans have gone awry? I've said it before – always expect things to go wrong and have a contingency plan. Success is about taking risks, but not about leaving yourself vulnerable to defeat. This assignment proved to be about more than just the task in hand.

Optimizing a location

It pays to know your territory, and to know where your competition is based. I was very interested to see the decisions the teams took and why.

Teamwork

By Task 9 our contenders knew each other's strengths and weaknesses quite well, but would that mean they could work together effectively as a team? It can be very difficult to communicate when you are split up on site, so careful planning, a clear strategy and effective delegation would be important. Several of the candidates cited this task as the most difficult of all.

Danger point: Stonewallers

This task wasn't without its challenges. In every organization there are people who take decisions that may not be theirs to make. This may be because they have not been fully briefed by senior management, or it may be because they are concerned by something that is a threat to their business at that particular point in time, or it may just be that they have a tendency towards self-importance. There is often no clear answer – but a stonewaller can cause frustration. There is no point in trying to deflate them; they will just dig their heels in deeper. In general, it is true to say that everything is negotiable, but on occasion you may come up against someone who simply doesn't want to shift their position. In that case, recognize that you are not going to get anywhere and change your tactics. Always have a contingency plan.

Business lesson: Flexibility

When you're out in the field your project management needs to be sound because communication can be difficult. The project manager has to be very well prepared, brief the team, be observant and be very ready to listen and react if things are going wrong.

Series 1 – Task 9 result

This was pitched as a marketing and promotional task, which caused Saira as a team leader some confusion. She thought that meant she didn't need to close sales on the day, and her team lost.

First Forte team leader:	**Saira**
Leading:	**James, Raj**
Impact team leader:	**Paul**
Leading:	**Miriam, Tim**

Winning strategy

The winning team had their fair share of challenges during this task. Having negotiated a deal for some marketing with the authorities at Tottenham Hotspur, they were forced to rethink their plans when permission was overturned at the last minute. Sheer desperation led them to sell one-on-one to fans attending the match, and as a result they beat the other team hands down. Sometimes obstacles are a blessing in disguise.

Winning team:	Impact
Impact:	Number of subscriptions: 704
First Forte:	Number of subscriptions: 468

In the boardroom: Saira took James and Raj with her to the boardroom. With only three team members left, none would escape my grilling. Saira had under-performed – had had an 'off day', as she described it. She argued strongly to be judged on her track record to date, not this task alone. Her sales skills were normally extremely strong, so I fired Raj instead. He was a talented candidate, but he let himself be used by others, and was too ready to tell me what he wasn't good at.

Fired: Raj

I'm glad she [Saira] stayed in because she has shined among everyone. So if it was me or her, I'm happy to be the fall guy.'

'In football you see players that look wonderful, very busy, running in and out, tackling, dribbling, falling over, getting up, tackling people well ... there's a lot of dancing going on, but where's the end product?'

SIR ALAN SUGAR – IN THE BOARDROOM

Business lesson 10: Sales presentations
— *Communicating the message*

Whatever medium you're using to sell a product, and whether you're selling face to face, on a podium, or via TV, it's important to present yourself well. If you're launching a product and giving a presentation to a customer or group of customers, you have to know exactly what the unique selling point of your product is and be able to get that message across quickly and clearly. The buyer needs to know what features will be of relevance to him or her. How is the product special? Why do they want it? How will it enhance their lives?

Presenting a sales pitch can be nerve-racking, so it's important to be well prepared. Waffling, pausing, apologizing or stuttering will leave your audience cold, whether you're on their doorstep or their TV screen. The pressure of performing in front of a live audience is high octane. You not only need the accurate information to present, but you also need the confidence and ability to perform in order to draw in your audience.

Telling your potential customer how well the product sells, how few you have left in stock, and how little time they have to make their decision to buy can often increase anticipation and speed up the buyer's decision-making process. In the case of luxury or the latest 'must have' items, the sheer exclusivity of the products and the fact that they are hard to come by can increase appeal (and the price tag).

The power of television

In the past, advertising on mainstream television has been critical to successful selling; but with so many TV channels now available, its power has been diluted tremendously. Most of the major brands do still invest in TV advertising, so one has to assume it still works, but it is no longer the be all and end all. The cost of producing an advert and hiring space on television is extremely high, and it is not always worth it in terms of subsequent sales.

Adverts on terrestrial TV were designed originally as short interruptions to programmes, but gradually became entertainments in their own right. With the advent of satellite TV, there is now an expanded opportunity for advertising. It was inevitable perhaps that a new breed of TV channel should develop that relies solely on selling products, and runs nothing but adverts all day. It says a lot about the public that people are keen to watch it. It's a kind of electronic trip to the market, the equivalent of shopping from a virtual catalogue. Instead of wandering around the stalls or shops, you can simply flick through lots of shopping channels, buying if you want to, and switching off if you don't.

This sort of electronic mail-order catalogue can be effective, but the user really needs to have the desire specifically to tune into such a channel. You've got to like shopping – and I mean really like shopping – and be willing to buy goods unseen.

Selling on television requires presentation skills rather than media skills. It's also vital how you present the information about the product – there's no point in waffling, time is money! We decided to put our remaining Series 1 candidates under fire to see how they coped in such a high-pressure environment. They could have learnt much of what they needed from the average street vendor or market trader shouting about their wares.

To give a good presentation you need to:
- Learn by doing.
- Be well prepared.
- Make sure you are looking in the right direction and not confuse people by giving mixed messages.
- Offer enough sales facts to entice a sale, but not so many that you bore your audience.
- Realize that timing is important.

- Have the ability to entertain and hold an audience.
- Anticipate questions that could be asked.

I wanted to see how the candidates presented themselves as well as the product; whether they were effective in closing a sale; how well they coped in front of the camera; and whether they were clear and concise or garbled. Crucially, I needed to see how well they pitched the sales facts. If they had the main ingredients, I would overlook imperfections.

Task 10: Presenting a sales pitch

CHALLENGE: To select a range of 'easy sell' products and pitch
             them to customers via a TV selling channel.

AIM: To sell as many units as possible and make the most
             profit in half an hour.

RULES AND REGULATIONS

☞   Each team received training in the art of media sales.

☞   The team members were given a choice of products.

☞   Each team had half an hour to sell three products. Each
    product carried a target price. The idea was to meet or
    exceed it.

☞   Each team had to choose different products from one
    another.

☞   The team with the highest profit was the winner.

SKILLS TESTED

☞   Ability to select the right products for the marketplace.

☞   Teamwork.

☞   Ability to hit sales targets.

☞   Ability to cope with pressure.

☞   Evolving a sales pitch that holds attention.

☞   Knowing when to change tack.

The skills used for this task were similar to those needed for previous tasks, but their application was different. Selecting the
right products for the market the candidates were trying to reach
would be an important element. I enjoyed this task, as I could
take part from the comfort of my own home!

Teamwork

The teams were small and working together tightly on this occasion. One team member would present on TV, while the other(s) would communicate essential details about the products via headphones. Coordinated and clear teamwork was critical in getting the right details to the presenter at the right time to get the message across to the home audience.

Ability to hit sales targets

Being a sales presenter on a television sales channel is a bit like being a puppet on a string: your team-mates are guiding your actions and you need to be ready to transform yourself at a moment's notice. They were selling yoghurt one minute, clothing the next, then jewellery, DIY tools ... you name it. To hit the targets the presenters needed to identify the essence of the product, communicate with the audience and create a buzz, just as a street vendor does when he's selling his wares — being loud, bold and giving customers plenty of information.

Ability to cope with pressure

The pressure in this instance related to the speed with which the vendor had to absorb information, and the clarity with which it had to be relayed to the viewers. This was a pretty intense activity, guaranteed to stretch each candidate's abilities in a way they had never had the opportunity to be tested before.

What interested me was how each candidate coped with the pressure — and I would say each of them handled it well on the day. Whether they would be able to cope with the pressure if they ended up in the boardroom was another matter ...

Evolving a sales pitch that holds attention

A successful sales pitch needs to be to the point, entertaining, appropriate, involve the audience, and communicate. The viewers need to be persuaded that they are being sold something that is going to improve their lives if they purchase it – in fact, they need and want this product! High-value goods need a greater depth of description and more facts than others. No one on the team had experience of selling in this very demanding environment. They had to learn pretty fast! Miriam took to it as if she had been doing it all her life, and was even offered a job afterwards.

Saira and James's style was more 'rough and ready', but ultimately proved more effective. Saira, from the control room, shouted louder and louder into James's earpiece as she directed him to follow her instructions on screen. The atmosphere was intense, but the result was successful, as well as entertaining. He followed her instructions to the letter and moved from sampling yoghurt with his fingers to donning a fleece 'wolf' jacket that wouldn't have looked out of place on a used-car salesman to demonstrating the pliability of a piece of foam bedding (the best sale of the day). He was constantly feeding sales information back to his TV audience, something that Miriam's team failed to do.

Knowing when to change tack

In any sales situation – from retail selling to a corporate deal to a car boot sale – you need to know when to push and when to step away from chasing a deal. In the true salesperson an instinct develops and you can tell when you've got a done deal. The beauty of watching shopping channels on TV is that the sales unfold in front of your eyes. You can tell almost immediately whether you have hooked the public interest by the running total of sales being made while you are on air, and you can change tack or change product in response. Of course, for that to work you need to have chosen the right products to sell in the first place. Saira had made some good choices for First Forte. Impact were not so lucky.

Danger point: Product selection

This was uncharted territory for our contestants. Few of them had ever watched a TV sales channel, and they had to learn fast. They had been told that some products would 'sell themselves' but that not all products lend themselves to on-screen sales. Some, such as jewellery, were too complicated to sell effectively. They needed to have asked some pretty astute questions of their advisers to make the right selection. Was the home audience male or female, interested in luxury holidays, DIY, gadgets, or bargain goods? Who would be watching? Home buyers or the trade? There were all kinds of potential pitfalls for our teams.

Business lesson: Teamwork

When the pressure is on, clarity is everything. It's critical that each individual knows what they are doing and is not over-loaded with information that leaves them dazed and confused. Had the team leaders got the balance right? And who was running the show?

Series 1 – Task 10 result

I was able to watch this task from the comfort of my own living room! The teams were to sell products live on TV. The team leaders became TV presenters; the others sourced products for them to present from a broad range on offer. The presenter was fed information about the products by their team-mates via an earpiece, live on air.

First Forte team leader:	James
Leading:	Saira

Impact team leader:	Miriam
Leading:	Paul, Tim

Winning strategy

In spite of Miriam's excellent presentation skills and Tim and Paul's tactical ability, James and Saira had the winning approach. Saira had chosen her products well, and won the day in spite of Tim and Paul trying to play a tactical game to get the upper hand. The combination of Saira's sales skill and James's enthusiastic presentational approach was highly effective. Saira used James as a mouthpiece, and he came across very well.

Winning team:	First Forte

First Forte:	Goods sold to a value of £5,407
Impact:	Goods sold to a value of £2,017

In the boardroom:	Miriam had no choice but to take both Tim and Paul with her to the boardroom. The result had surprised me initially because Miriam's presentation was excellent. However, Saira's sales skills and forceful direction had enabled James to do a very credible job of selling a better selection of products and giving more sales information to the public. Tim, and Paul especially, had played their part in Miriam's team's failure. A ploy to out-manoeuvre Saira in product selection had backfired as they made poorer choices than she had. Nor had they fed enough sales information to Miriam during her presentation. It was a hard call as I thought highly of all the candidates. I decided to fire Miriam, on the basis that she should have managed her team better and not allowed them to direct her at the same time. It was not a popular decision, but I called it as I saw it at the time.
Fired:	Miriam
	'I think it was Paul's time to go … I'm glad to see that it wasn't an easy decision for Sir Alan, that is somewhat flattering, [but] I think it was product choice that was more responsible.'

'Fair? Fair? I'll give you fair! The only 'fair'
I'll be giving you is your train fare home!'
SIR ALAN SUGAR – IN THE BOARDROOM

Business lesson 11: Interviewing –
Interviews and how to survive them

Every job interview at every level should aim to assess the following:

- Skills and experience appropriate to the business.
- Personal characteristics.
- Whether the shortlist candidates will fit the organization.
- Whether the preferred candidate has the 'wow' factor.

The candidates who reach this stage of the competition have been on a fast-track business journey. They have been tested beyond their normal limits, have overcome immense challenges, have learnt a great deal, have come to know each other very well, and have developed their team skills very effectively.

Now, however, it is up to them as individuals. Their CVs will be read, reviewed, inspected, dissected and questioned – hard. If there are any cracks, we now have enough inside knowledge of their attitude, skills and behaviour to be able to find them!

An interview is a two-way process. It is primarily about the interviewer(s) deciding whether you have the right skills, abilities and personality for their business culture. Equally, however, it is about the candidates deciding whether the role, culture and scope of the job are going to be beneficial in building their careers.

A successful interview and the ability to sell yourself draws on many of the skills outlined in Part 1 of this book. Do you think like a winner? Can you lead from the front? How hungry are you – for the job, as well as personal success? Can you sell yourself as you would any other product you believe in? What's your motive for applying in the first place? What have you got to offer?

At the end of the day you are going through a formal buying and selling process, and the buyer needs to decide whether they want to keep you, or whether they will wish they'd made a different style of purchase once the deal is done. Just as you would take time to get to know a product you are selling, so too you need to know yourself.

Task 11: Undergoing boardroom interviews

CHALLENGE: To be selected as one of the Series 2
             semi-finalists.
AIM: To survive intensive high-pressure questioning.

QUALITIES ASSESSED:
- ☛ Intelligence.
- ☛ Ability to perform well at interviews.
- ☛ Ability to sell yourself.
- ☛ Nerves under pressure.
- ☛ Coherence.
- ☛ Suitability for the company culture.

The remaining candidates are put through a whole day of gruelling interviews with my trusted advisers: Nick Hewer and Margaret Mountford; Bordan Tkachuk, CEO of Viglen; Claude Litner, Amstrad Group adviser and Paul Kemsley, founding director of Rock Investments. During these hard, tense and personal sessions, the candidates' CVs are dissected, any possible exaggerations highlighted, and their performance in previous tasks thoroughly examined.

Intelligence
In life, as in business, there are different kinds of intelligence. That is not meant to be philosophical; it's a simple statement of fact. A theological scholar with several degrees and diplomas is undoubtedly intelligent, but would not survive much further than the reception desk in one of our organizations! A street trader in London, Manchester or Glasgow for example has a different kind of savvy: they have street-smart intelligence and

highly tuned survival skills – very useful in business. I am looking for someone who has the demeanour and presence to operate at a senior level, but who is street smart as well.

Whether you are interviewer or interviewee, I would recommend being absolutely honest about your corporate culture and the kind of intelligence you need before you begin the interview process.

Ability to perform well at interviews

We always talk about performing well at interviews, and there's no doubt that in many cases the performance can be greater than the substance! What is needed is not a false façade that the interviewers then have to unpeel like a many-layered parcel, but clarity, honesty and well-prepared and calm presentation. The interviewers are not there to get to know you as a friend would over a long period of time; they need to be able to assess quickly whether you would be good for the commercial future of the organization.

The Internet, dozens of books and myriad courses exist to tell you the obvious:

- Make sure you have researched the company before you attend the interview. They are taking the trouble to read about you, and you are of no interest to them if you don't know who they are or why you're there.
- Look smart. You are being judged. It doesn't matter that everyone else in the company is walking around in jeans and trainers. You are there to sell something valuable: you are there to sell yourself.
- When you go into a shop and you're making a purchase, do you buy the product in the damaged box, or do you hunt for the one in pristine packaging? It doesn't matter that, damaged or undamaged, either box will go straight into the

bin once you get home, nor that the product inside the damaged box is exactly the same as the one in the pristine box. You are making an investment and you want perfection. Employers are the same. They are looking for the perfect candidate. If you haven't ironed your shirt, or your shoes are down at heel, they will wonder what else you are likely to neglect in business.

 Speak clearly and slow down: you need to be heard as well as understood. If you bombard your interviewer with too much information at once, they will be overwhelmed and have to work too hard to ensure they have understood your core strengths. Look at the person you are speaking to and ensure that you are giving each other undivided attention.

Be aware of the characteristics required for the role you are applying for, and be ready to talk about your strengths, your weaknesses and your personal achievements in life in relation to the skills the interviewer is looking for.

Have the courage to be yourself at all times.

Ability to sell yourself

It is important to be able to give a good account of yourself in life – not just at interview, but when operating in business both generally and socially. As mentioned earlier, this does not mean putting on an act, but it does mean presenting a confidence and self-assurance that others can rely on. You have to know your skills and know yourself. I'm not recommending years of psychotherapy here, although there's nothing wrong with that if it's needed; I simply mean that the more you are true to yourself, the more you will be believed, and the more likely you are to get the job. After that, the normal rules of selling apply: keep it focused, keep it clear, keep to the point.

Nerves under pressure

I see adrenalin as a good thing. Adrenalin is what feeds your energy levels and provides a sense of urgency in life. Usually, the only time adrenalin really becomes detrimental in an interview situation is when a candidate is badly prepared.

Of course, some interviewers adopt very direct tactics, and more senior-level interviews can be extremely intense and personal. The thing to do is not to take them personally. You are there to inform the interviewer, and they are there to decide whether you and your skills are right for the job they are offering. It is a buying and selling process – it's not personal!

Coherence

It is amazing how many people will begin to babble incoherently when they feel they are in the spotlight. Stop. Pause. Think. Before answering any question, ensure that you know why it is being asked, and the likely impact of your answer. Coherence is critical to making a strong impression. It implies self-assurance, intelligent thinking, an ability to think on your feet, and calmness under pressure.

Suitability for the company culture

Once again, it comes down to research in advance of the interview itself. Find out as much as you can. If you don't like what you see, don't waste anyone's time. However, if you're potentially interested and have further questions, or you're ecstatic about the opportunity and are desperate for the job, do your research and, in the words of your average boy scout, 'Be prepared'.

Danger points: False pretences and favouritism

As a candidate, trying to be someone you are not is always a major mistake. Never say things just to impress.

As an interviewer, deciding purely on the basis of personality is always a mistake. If you are tempted to choose someone simply because you like their company, seek a second opinion because you are likely to be blind to some of their faults.

Business lesson: Listen to advice

As a candidate, the best way to be hired is to be well prepared, and to be aware of what you can bring to the company in both the commercial and personal sense.

As an interviewer, never ask for advice unless you are willing to listen to it, and always ask the advice of those you trust. Add the knowledge of others to your own knowledge and experience, and make an informed decision, not an impulsive one. Although it sounds contradictory, it is much easier to fire people before you hire them – that is, before they have become part of your team!

Series 1 – Task 11 result

I brought in a team of trusted advisers to undertake incisive interviews with the candidates. Margaret Mountford and Nick Hewer knew the candidates well and had seen their strengths and weaknesses during the previous 10 weeks. My work colleagues Bordan Tkachuk, CEO of Viglen, Claude Littner, Amstrad group adviser, and Paul Kemsley, founding director of Rock Investments gave me a more objective view.

Just four candidates remained – two from each of the teams. Things were getting very tense.

First Forte: **James, Saira**

Impact: **Paul, Tim**

Winning strategy – Series 1

In this task the only strategy that would work was to be honest, enthusiastic and clear in intention. It was hard for the candidates because no matter how good they had been up until now, two of them would be going home. This was a job interview, and cultural fit with my companies was more important than personal achievement to date. I knew I needed an apprentice, not a business adviser.

WINNING SEMI-FINALISTS

As chance would have it, the chosen two were from different teams. Tim (from Impact) got through for his raw enthusiasm, intelligence and passion for the opportunity. Saira (from First Forte) was selected for her proven sales ability, energy and pure determination.

In the boardroom: There is no point in asking the opinions of others if you are not going to listen to what they have to say. There was a mixed body of response from my advisers. Some felt Saira was a genuinely passionate candidate, strong on sales, but untested in a broader field; others felt that James was personable and highly talented, while some thought his motives for wanting the job were unclear; Tim was favoured by many, and seen as an undiscovered gem, but lacked commercial nous, so was a gamble and would need coaching; Paul was a maverick with strong sales skills, and knew the property market, but he seemed to cast himself in more of an advisory than an Apprentice role, which was not what I needed.

Fired: James and Paul

'I gave it my best shot ... I think it is slightly disappointing that people didn't break through their perception of me and my aspirations. Maybe he just thought that I just wasn't right, personality-wise, for him or his team. And I respect that.'

'Yes, sometimes I am tough in my approach, but I definitely don't see it as aggressive ... a good businessman has to be aggressive. Sir Alan never made a £700 million fortune by being soft ... He said in one or two boardrooms that there were elements in me that he saw years ago in himself ... but obviously that didn't count ... because he fired me.'

Business lesson 12: Project management
— *The art of planning and leadership*

This task is the culmination of 12 weeks' intensive effort. A business journey unlike any other, it allows our intrepid candidates to develop skills, try new business areas, develop their management and leadership skills, and demonstrate to me that they have what it takes to make it within one of my organizations.

In the final event, each of our two finalists is on their own. They are able to select three former team-mates to join their team, but the business planning and decisions are up to them as individuals. There is no more 'we'; now it is all 'I, me, my' in a test of leadership, project management, time management, financial acumen and decision-making ability. This task is pure business at the sharp end.

The issues that raise their head and the challenges that our two finalists have to overcome are not dissimilar to those that take place in every office across the country every day. The location may be different, but not the issues involved:

- Strategic vision is a must in a business leader. There is more to business growth than short-term profit. Long-term viability and repeat business are also essential.
- The ability to plan ahead, anticipate problems, to stay calm under pressure, delegate effectively and follow through are all vital skills for anyone who wants to be a business success.
- People skills are also important. You can't achieve everything on your own, so you need the loyalty, enthusiasm and respect of your team. Respect has to be earned, not demanded, and our team leaders know that their support people no longer have anything personal to gain from the contest – apart from the feel-good factor of helping a former team-mate to win. This makes the team leader vulnerable. Can they trust each of their advisers not to sabotage the project out of disappointment?

☛ Finally, the ability to multi-task, think on your feet, be flexible and change direction if necessary (without making panic decisions) are what sets a winner apart from the pack.

In Series 1, the team leaders were town planner and salesperson Saira, and HR leader and London Underground employee, Tim.

Task 12: Project-managing an event

CHALLENGE: To successfully organize and manage an event on a Thames riverboat.

AIM: To project-manage the event from start to finish, to give it a recognizable theme, to brief and motivate a personally chosen team and to make some profit.

RULES AND REGULATIONS

☞ The two finalists each had two days to plan an event, recruit all necessary staff and design a venue.

☞ They had two days trying to fill the venue with fee-paying guests.

☞ They each had £5,000 seed money.

☞ The event had to have food, drink, entertainment and a recognizable theme.

☞ Candidates were judged on their overall success in managing all aspects of this project: logistics, budget, promotion and marketing of the event, customer satisfaction, staff management, creativity and profitability.

☞ The winner was the candidate who made the most money.

SKILLS TESTED

☞ Business management.

☞ People management.

☞ The art of delegation.

☞ Communicating.

☞ Leadership.

When it comes to event management, the key factors are as follows.

Business management

- Vision – clearly defined and easily communicated.
- Planning – every aspect of the project broken into manageable tasks.
- Networking – who do you know who can help you deliver your idea? Involve them from the early stages and make sure they feel appreciated.
- Budgeting – start with your target price, your necessary profit margin and work back to costs.
- Implementation – through effective delegation and third-party expertise.
- Marketing – to make your market aware that you have something they will want to buy.
- Selling – the cornerstone of success. Without effective sales you will not deliver a successful project.
- Delivery – in the case of an event, delivery is in two main stages:
  1. Delivering the project to launch.
  2. Ensuring that your paying guests have the time of their lives.

People management

- Motivating – especially your trusted inner team, who will then, in turn, motivate others.
- Delegating – once you have drawn up your plan, delegate as much as possible to able people whom you can trust to deliver.
- Communicating – clearly, directly and frequently. Keep in touch throughout the process and make sure all is on track.
- Leading – from the front and with confidence, even if your style is instinctively consensual. Unless you show leadership you will not command respect, and unless you command respect you will not be kept properly informed.

How do you motivate your team? When you're on a limited budget, pay can seem like a major hurdle to achieving your ends, but the truth is, contrary to popular belief, pay is not the main motivator in people's choice of work; there are many non-financial incentives as well:

- Quality of work.
- A need to belong as part of a team.
- A sense of achievement.
- Recognition of success and effort.
- The opportunity to progress in career.
- Personal fulfilment.
- Increased responsibility and autonomy.

All of these are cheaper than a pay rise and can add a great deal to the effectiveness of a project.

A successful team wants to like its leader; the individuals enjoy sharing in the success of the team and will spark new ideas that will lead to a more financially successful business.

The art of delegation
Delegation, as I have said before, is not about letting go; it is about planning in advance and communicating throughout. Delegation is the equivalent of a brain extension. You are using someone else's brain to deliver your thoughts. So don't fall asleep on the job. You can't deliver if you're not concentrating – even with all the brains at your disposal!

Communicating
Communication is not about breathing down everyone's neck, nor is it about waiting to be told. Communication is about using your nose to sense what might go wrong before it happens and

to see it off at the pass; it is about keeping in touch with your key players and ensuring that they share your vision, are on side and are delegating effectively themselves; it is also about being seen by the rest of the people involved in the project, being available if required for important issues, and keeping everyone informed in practical terms about what is going on. Save the flattery and the niceties for later. Acknowledge and appreciate when people have delivered, but keep things moving.

Leadership

It is human nature to want a role model, and to want to work for someone you respect. Never underestimate what you are teaching people about yourself and about management when you are in a leadership role. For good or bad, you will be judged and assessed, so you may as well be a confident, motivating and well-organized leader that your team can respect rather than one who is forever remembered for incompetence and ingratitude.

Event management is incredibly challenging because you are dealing with people en masse who have paid to have a good time. There will be divas, drunkards, acrimonious couples and everybody's uncle, as well as party-goers, grandmothers, birthday girls and wedding parties. You will have to deal with the vagaries of the weather, the challenges presented by caterers, drivers, domestic staff and probably the police too if things get out of hand!

I had no doubt that the task would stretch the candidates to the utmost, and likewise no doubt that they had the ability to deliver. It was a spectacular task and one that was a credit to all involved. No matter who I appointed to help run one of my companies, I was quite certain that both final contestants were outstanding individuals who would go far.

Series 1 – Task 12 result

This final task was all about personal vision, team management and business focus. Predictably, both team leaders selected their previous team-mates to work with.

First Forte: Saira
Leading: James, Paul, Raj

Impact: Tim
Leading: Ben, Miriam, Sebastian

Winning strategy

Tim and Saira took completely different approaches to the tasks. Saira chose the 'Elizabethan', a traditional paddle-steamer, and opted to for a tried-and-tested style of event, with the costs underwritten by sponsorship money. She hosted a lively party to launch a new brand of Californian wine. Saira had the edge in terms of profitability and sales instinct, having the sense to control the amount of free wine that was being given to guests in order to encourage them to spend more at the bar. The thematic elements of the event were understated and her management style alienated one member of her team for a time, but she succeeded in making the evening a great success.

Tim opted for the 'Natacia', a modern river cruiser, because it had the equivalent of a catwalk. He wanted to host an event that would impress, so put together a full-blown fashion show. He did not make a profit on the night – and had a number of obstacles to overcome – but showed me aspects of his business nature that I hadn't seen before and demonstrated his potential by taking a longer term, strategic approach to profit. He had considered other ways of making money from the event that would also lead to future business. His attention to detail was impressive – there was no doubt he had the loyalty and goodwill of his team.

Both teams had trouble selling tickets for the events, but all had a good time on the night. Saira made significantly more profit, but Tim hosted the more spectacular event.

The winner:	Tim (Impact)	
Impact:	Spent £2,200	Profit £0
First Forte:	Spent £0	Profit £800

In the boardroom: This was the most difficult decision of the series. Saira's business sense had delivered profit. Tim's vision and determination had resulted in the more spectacular event and a business plan that could, in theory, bring in long-term profit, but his profit margin was next to nothing.

Saira's choice to have Paul on her team was interesting as they had similar characters and had clashed in a work context throughout the series. Fortunately, Saira also had diplomat James on her team to save the day when things got out of hand.

It was a question of solid sales skills versus a 'rough diamond'; a feisty go-getter versus a deter-mined 'Mr Nice Guy'. We filmed two different endings, so the two candidates had as long as the viewers to find out who the final winner was.

Hired: Tim

The Outcome

The chart overleaf summarizes the progress of Series 1 candidates from week 1 to week 12. Retrospect is a wonderful thing. It allows you to see things in greater perspective, and it also allows 'instant experts' who weren't involved at the front line to think they could have done a better job! In my experience, retrospect rarely alters my view about my original decision – which would have been made based upon knowledge, understanding and instinct about the situation at the time – but it is a useful way of taking stock and making sense of the detail.

I made several controversial firing decisions during the course of the first series, and will no doubt make more during the second series. There are those who felt that volatile candidates, such as Paul or Saira, should have left earlier, or that others, such as Ben, Raj, James or Miriam, were judged unfairly. That may be true. They were all talented people, and not every task allowed their talent to shine. However, as you will find when watching the next series, there is more than one way to reach the same outcome in a situation. Even had certain firing decisions been made differently, the eventual outcome would have been the same. *The Apprentice* is not a competition – it is a 12-week job interview. I was confident that Tim was an outstanding candidate and one that met the needs of Amstrad most closely; the evidence in retrospect makes it a certainty.

	TASK 1	TASK 2	TASK 3	TASK 4	TASK 5	TASK 6	
Winning team	IMPACT	IMPACT	IMPACT	IMPACT	FIRST FORTE	FIRST FORTE	
Tim	WINNING TEAM LEADER		Moves to First Forte	Losing team leader			
Saira	Losing team leader		Moves to Impact			Chosen for boardroom	
Paul					Chosen for boardroom	Losing team leader	
James				WINNING TEAM LEADER	Moves to First Forte		
Miriam		Chosen for boardroom				WINNING TEAM LEADER	
Raj		WINNING TEAM LEADER					
Ben			Moves to First Forte. Chosen for boardroom				
Sebastian			Moves to First Forte		WINNING TEAM LEADER		
Rachel			Moves to Impact		Losing team leader	FIRED	
Matthew			WINNING TEAM LEADER		FIRED		
Adele		Chosen for boardroom	Losing team leader	RESIGNS/ FIRED			
Miranda	Chosen for boardroom		FIRED				
Lindsay		Losing team leader FIRED					
Adenike	FIRED						
NOTES			Saira and Rachel move to Impact. Tim, Ben and Sebastian move to First Forte	Boardroom cancelled as Adele walks	James moves to First Forte		

TASK 7	TASK 8	TASK 9	TASK 10	TASK 11	TASK 12
IMPACT	FIRST FORTE	IMPACT	FIRST FORTE	(INTERVIEWS)	IMPACT
Moves to Impact			Chosen for boardroom	SEMI-FINALIST	TIM IS HIRED AS *THE APPRENTICE*
		Losing team leader		SEMI-FINALIST	FINALIST
Moves to Impact	Chosen for boardroom	WINNING TEAM LEADER	Chosen for boardroom	FIRED	Returns to join Saira's team
Losing team leader		Chosen for boardroom	WINNING TEAM LEADER	FIRED	Returns to join Saira's team
Moves to Impact	Chosen for boardroom		Losing team leader FIRED		Returns to join Tim's team
Chosen for boardroom	WINNING TEAM LEADER	FIRED			Returns to join Saira's team
Moves to Impact WINNING TEAM LEADER	Losing team leader FIRED				Returns to join Tim's team
Moves to First Forte FIRED					Returns to join Tim's team
Sir Alan separates Paul and Saira. Asks them to reshuffle the teams					

chapter six

A YEAR IN THE LIFE OF TIM CAMPBELL

Tim Campbell will be familiar to all of you who watched the first series as the worthy winner of *The Apprentice*, seeing off the combined talents of his fellow candidates. It has been a challenging year for Tim and he has stepped up to the plate admirably;

'The reason I wanted to win The Apprentice was to be taken out of my comfort zone.'

he manages Integra (www.integra-skincare.com), a new division of the company, and recently launched a new range of women's beauty products, putting into practice all the skills learnt on the TV series. He was interviewed about his experiences during the past year.

Q. Has the opportunity to become The Apprentice been all you hoped for and expected?

A. The reality of working at Amstrad as The Apprentice has been brilliant. The experience has been even more than I hoped for. A modern apprenticeship means learning by observation. Frequently the best you can hope for on a so-called apprenticeship is to be given the desk jobs, filing and other tasks that no one else wants to do. There is rarely any scope to develop or shine. The way that Sir Alan manages, however, is by empowering you to develop your skills from the outset. If you believe you've got the talent, and he trusts that talent, he'll just let you go for it. It's one of the reasons I respect him as a leader and a manager.

'Respect for others breeds respect. It's a concept that was an important part of my upbringing and it's my choice to conduct business in the same way.'

Sir Alan's empowering approach was clear from my first morning at Amstrad when I arrived to find an email from him outlining a task and telling me to get on with it. That was it. His approach was: 'Navigate your way around the company; these are the people you need to speak to; come back later and tell me what you've done.' It was potentially a 'sink or swim' situation and I was well aware there would be no special favours just because of the television series. He put the emphasis on my own drive to succeed, although I knew I could count on his support. He was saying 'Go out and show me what you can do in the first instance, but if you need anything, come back and ask me.' His approach was brilliant from my point of view. It meant I felt free to go out and make my own way, with access to his guidance when necessary. He kept an eye on me of course, and would come down to the office to ask, 'Where are you now and what are you up to?' or to advise, 'Well, maybe you should reconsider this bit' or praise, 'That's really, really good.'

I think Sir Alan's TV persona belies his managerial style. Of course he's a bit of a taskmaster in driving for results, and that's very important. But the fact is that he harnesses the skills and resources of his team very, very well. He is extremely good at motivating and getting the most out of people: not, as some might think, through a 'climate of fear' because that just wouldn't work. I have talked to a lot of people at Amstrad and the majority have worked here for 5–10 years. You don't retain people for that long if you are feared.

I love the responsibility of running my own division and I don't really feel as if I have a job because it's not like a normal job. This is not a 9–5 situation. I'm now responsible at whatever hour. I've got the brilliant support of Amstrad and the team and the company; but this division is mine and I have to make things happen.

Q. Have you had to try to overcome your image as Mr Nice Guy in order to be respected?

A. I think there is a false perception in business that you have to be quite harsh and horrid to people in order to succeed, to avoid people taking advantage of you, but in reality there is room for many different styles. My individual style is not about coercion; it's about cooperation and treating people with respect. I have built on my reputation for integrity as an individual. It's a key element in my business dealings and how I conduct myself in the business environment.

Respect for others breeds respect. It's a concept that was an important part of my upbringing and it's my choice to conduct business in the same way. I want to be remembered and regarded as a respected businessman because this is more than a job opportunity for me – I'm trying to build a legacy, not just for the company and the division, but for me and my family as well. It's very important to me that I am judged on my own merits, not as someone who won a television contest. In the long term that's not what I want to be remembered for.

'For me, The Apprentice is about focusing on doing something you love, while making sure that what you love is going to be profitable as well as self-fulfilling.'

Q. What have been the triumphs and challenges of the last year?

A. My life during the last year has changed completely. It is totally different. My greatest triumph, involving many challenges, was getting my face care system product to market. On 20 September, after a year of concentrated effort, I stood in front of 30–50 journalists and launched my first product to the media. In spite of some of the journalists being pretty harsh, the whole event was great fun. It has been an amazing year.

Everything relating to the system starts with my own doing and decision-making. I've had to direct everything: from the colour scheme to deciding which buttons should go where on the machine, from choosing which topical application creams should come with the product to what the website looks like. Getting the product to market has given me a phenomenal sense of achievement – and that's a great feeling.

'Never be too proud to ask others for the benefit of their advice and knowledge.'

Everything in business boils down to three things for me. These are things I've learnt over the years and which have been reinforced since working with Sir Alan:

- The first thing you need is a market. As long as you've got customers who want something, you have a chance to make money.
- Then you need a profit margin: whatever you manufacture or sell, you've got to be able to sell it for more than you made it for.
- Finally, you've got to distinguish yourself from the competition.

I've got all three of those elements in my product; and I kept focused on them throughout the product's development. There's no mythical solution for success in business, and the perception that only a few people can achieve success is false. As long as you've got those three core elements in place, you have a chance.

I think what really distinguishes peo- ple who succeed from those who don't is how much energy they're willing to put into achieving success. I have had a lot to prove in my new role. There were many differing views in terms of who should

'Focus on a clear belief that you are going to be successful.'

have won the first series of *The Apprentice*. I had to justify and prove to Sir Alan for my own benefit that he'd made the right choice. It was personal. I wasn't going to do that by sitting around and doing nothing or waiting to be told what to do. So getting my product to market was very, very important.

Integra Skincare has been launched as part of Sir Alan's new Sir Alan Sugar Enterprise Scheme. It was one thing to get my product to market, but it was quite another to gain his endorsement. I'd like to see other people getting involved in business and having their chance to become successful entrepreneurs too.

Q. What would you say to other aspiring Apprentices – both those in the series and those in the 'outside world' – who want to reach the top in business?

A. First I would say, be clear about what makes success happen in business. There is great emphasis on entrepreneurship in the media at the moment, which is brilliant in terms of focusing on individu- als' self-belief, effort and determination to succeed on their own. But this sometimes confuses our understanding of what business actually is. If you're an entrepreneur, you need to think of yourself first and foremost as a business person. Whether you're in business because you love what you do, or because it's your heart's desire to run your own company, you need to remember first of all that you're there to make money. Otherwise there's no point in starting because your business won't last very long and you'll end up in a lot of debt.

For me, *The Apprentice* is about focusing on doing something you love, while making sure that what you love is going to be profitable as well as self-fulfilling. There's no point in developing a product that no one wants to buy. Profitability is the bottom line: that's the way the world is. The good thing is that focusing on the bottom line makes business decisions easier to make. What I would say to aspiring Apprentices is: focus totally on what you want to do. Research it until you can't research it any more.

After Sir Alan asked me to develop a product for the health and beauty market, I spent the first couple of months doing pure desk research and going out to speak to people until I knew my market inside out. I wanted to find out exactly what the people in this market actually wanted – what they needed, what their habits were and what demographics they fitted. Then all I had to do was to give them something they already wanted. Market understanding helps profitability. That's the key for the Apprentices.

On a personal level, I believe there were two characteristics that got me through to the final of the show. The first is never being too proud to ask others for the benefit of their advice and knowledge: it saves a whole heap of trouble, and

> *'If it's meant to be it will be, but you've got to make it happen.'*

avoids you having to reinvent the wheel. The second is focusing on a clear belief that you are going to be successful. I don't mean a blind, lemming-style belief. It's more about understanding your positive qualities, understanding where you want to get to and focusing on your goal. If anything comes in your way to hinder your progress, navigate your way around it rather than seeing it as an immovable object. My belief in life is, 'If it's meant to be, it will be, but you've got to make it happen'. Whatever happens, you will learn from the process and the outcome, and will be a better person for it.

The reason I wanted to win *The Apprentice* was to be taken out of my comfort zone. I wanted to be taken away from the mundane 9–5 world of being a small cog in a large wheel. Sir Alan facilitated that and now I am learning new things and meeting new challenges every day. It's a wonderful way to learn the business of business and I hope I will still be working at Amstrad in 40 years' time.

CONCLUSION

Fired or hired?

Firing people is not pleasant. You'd be an iron-cold person if you said it doesn't matter. Whether someone has been with the company for two weeks or 20 years, it's never easy telling them they've got to go. There are times when it's actually heartbreaking to deliver that news, but it has to be done. It's business, not personal.

On the other hand, there are certain types of people I have no trouble firing: the lazy, the incompetent, the disloyal...

Before shooting each series of *The Apprentice* I was sure I would find it difficult to say 'I'm sorry, you're fired' to at least one of the candidates. I was also convinced that it would be a relief to say 'You're fired' to some of the others. We were bound to get to a situation, especially towards the end, when those words would be personally shattering for a would-be Apprentice. But the nature of this exercise is that only one of the finalists can win.

I was looking forward to the moment when instead of saying 'You're fired' I could finally say...

'You're hired!'

A final word...

When I was starting out I was on my own. I had no mentor, no guidance, nothing. It was sheer hard work. But a successful entrepreneur cannot survive in isolation. It's important to know who your business partners are and who's in your support team. I began to employ staff when the operation became too big – when it became necessary to provide warehousing, production and packaging that I had no time or inclination to do myself.

Any young person today who feels they want to start a business on their own and wants to deal with products that cost a lot to develop and a lot to manufacture won't be able to go it alone – it's as simple as that. It's a fact of modern life. It's my view that before you set up on your own it is important to get some commercial experience. Once you've worked for somebody and have decided whether or not you like that work, you'll be closer to understanding the industry and seeing the opportunities that exist within it.

Once you've settled down to doing what you like, and have acquired some experience, at that point only will you say, 'I tell you what – I'm going to do this for myself.' So before you leap out of bed one Monday morning shouting, 'I want to run my own airline', take the time to understand what running an airline means. Take the time to understand the industry infrastructure, see if you like it, see whether you have a desire for it, and only then begin to think about running the show yourself.

That's what happened to me. As a kid, I was always interested in electronics, and I would buy crystal sets from a shop in Hackney. I suppose the tape-recorder company I first worked for attracted me because I already had an interest and an understanding. When I first started my business making amplifiers and hi-fi units it was literally a cottage industry. I made them in my garage or workshop. That was the way things happened in those days. Michael Dell, too, started off by assembling computers in his garage. But that's not possible now.

If you want to be competitive in the marketplace, you have to come in with the leading-edge technology. There are no longer any people like Stanley Kalms (now Lord Kalms) or Jack Cohen in the retail trade. There are very few people like me around either. It's a new wave, a new world.

Although it's more difficult these days, there are ways of getting there eventually. Experience is the key.

The UK is no longer a country of manufacturers. We're traders (we've always been traders), we have service-industry organizations, and, unfortunately, over the last 10–15 years we've seen people able to make money out of nothing, out of vapourware, out of talk, out of expectation rather than product. It has been demoralizing sometimes for a hardworking person like Arnold Weinstock, who founded GEC, to suddenly see a dot.com company enter the marketplace out of nowhere and within minutes have a market capitalization far larger than his company's. Although demoralizing, it also tells a story. It tells a story of the marketplace that you're dealing with, it tells a story of what the market is about, and it tells a story of how we have adapted dangerously towards investing in hype. The danger is that more companies will be hyped up, expectations will be hyped up, and profits don't seem to mean anything any more. Traditional ways of making money are becoming meaningless now.

The old-fashioned trader and the old-style manufacturer have gone from this country, and I suppose you've got to be realistic and understand it. At my age I find that very difficult to accept, but I recognize it and try to deal with it. I do so by employing young people to run the businesses for me.

People younger than me understand the people we're interfacing with, who we're trying either to buy from or sell to. They can enjoy playing the game, but get from me, I hope, the instinct for when to go in for the kill. They can have 17 meetings with 15 people, sit and listen to the nonsense, talk about the spreadsheets, discuss the theory, but at the end of the day what we want is an order. At the end of the day what we want is to buy or sell something. Unfortunately, it's not quite as simple as it was 35 years ago, and to get those goals I've had to learn to be far more patient.

Starting a business on your own is a great challenge. In my case, I just set out to be independent. It is the small businesses up and down the country, employing anything from two to 20 people, who are the true backbone of the country. There are some great success stories in Britain, and we need a lot more.

There is nothing more satisfying than the euphoria of success, that first week in which you earn more than you ever did when you worked for someone else. And when you employ someone, you are serving the country's economy as well as yourself.

You need to start a business as young as you possibly can, before you get yourself too committed with mortgages or children, and while you can still afford to take the gamble and see whether you can make it out there on your own. You must have a gambling instinct and be adventurous. You can afford to while you're young. Later on, when you have commitments, being adventurous is irresponsible. So be bold. If you're thinking about it, do it! Set a target date!

Only you will understand the buzz that comes from achieving something on your own. In a funny way, the money takes second place, and what I've found really interests me now is helping others on their way.

APPENDIX

You be the interviewer

Can you assess key personal characteristics and business performance to judge which candidate will be the winner? On the following
pages there is a list showing the order of the Series 2 tasks and a chart
that you can photocopy then fill in each week during the TV series,
noting your own scores for each of the candidates. Assess the candidates' performance each week on these key personal characteristics
and entrepreneurial business strengths, and give them a score from
0 to 10. The scores you give and your assessment of the candidates'
performance during each task might provide you with useful pointers
for your own future.

Series 2 Task Order

While the skills tested in the tasks remain fundamentally the same as those in Series 1, the contexts for them, and the order in which they are tackled, are slightly different.

Street selling – negotiation, selling, innovation

Product design – understanding a market, creativity, pitching

Discount buying – negotiating

Profit margins – innovation, team management, customer service

Designing an advertising campaign – market awareness, creativity, pitching and presentation

Selling and closing a deal – selling, promotion

Retail management – selling in a retail environment, brand awareness, market understanding, promotion

Trade selling – selling business-to-business, promotions, pitching and negotiation

Sales negotiation – understanding of particular market, communicating the message

Innovative money-making – creativity, influencing skills, commercial awareness, personality, negotiation

Interviews – motivation, self-belief, presentation and influencing skills, keeping calm under pressure

Event management – planning, team management, leadership, motivational skills, commercial savvy, tenacity, imagination, strategic awareness, charisma

SECOND SERIES INTERVIEWING CHART (Marks out of ten)	Alexa	Ansell	Benedict	Jo	Karen	
ORIGINALITY						
FOCUS						
DRIVE						
CHARISMA						
LEADERSHIP SKILLS						
ABILITY TO PLAN						
DELEGATION SKILLS						
TEAMWORKING						
SELLING SKILLS						
FLEXIBILTY						
COOL UNDER PRESSURE						
COURAGE						
STREET SMART						
BUSINESS SAVVY						
TOTAL SCORE						

	Mani	Michelle	Nargis	Paul	Ruth	Samuel	Sharon	Syed	Tuan

SECOND SERIES FIRED OR HIRED CHART	Alexa	Ansell	Benedict	Jo	Karen	
No. of times as team leader (No. of wins as team leader in brackets)						
No. of times on winning team						
No. of times on losing team						
No. of times in boardroom						
TASK 1 STREET SELLING						
Into the boardroon/Who's fired?						
TASK 2 PRODUCT DESIGN						
Into the boardroon/Who's fired?						
TASK 3 DISCOUNT BUYING						
Into the boardroon/Who's fired?						
TASK 4 PROFIT MARGINS						
Into the boardroon/Who's fired?						
TASK 5 AD CAMPAIGN						
Into the boardroon/Who's fired?						
TASK 6 CLOSING THE DEAL						
Into the boardroon/Who's fired?						
TASK 7 RETAIL MANAGEMENT						
Into the boardroon/Who's fired?						
TASK 8 SELLING TO THE TRADE						
Into the boardroon/Who's fired?						
TASK 9 SALES NEGOTIATION						
Into the boardroon/Who's fired?						
TASK 10 INNOVATIVE MONEY-MAKING						
Into the boardroon/Who's fired?						
TASK 11 BOARD INTERVIEWS						
Into the boardroon/Who's fired?						
TASK 12 EVENT MANAGEMENT						
Into the boardroon/Who's fired?						

	Mani	Michelle	Nargis	Paul	Ruth	Samuel	Sharon	Syed	Tuan	Winning Team

INDEX